When FOOTBALL *Was* FOOTBALL

WEST HAM

© Haynes Publishing, 2015

The right of Iain Dale to be identified as the author of this Work has been asserted
by him in accordance with the Copyright, Designs & Patents Act 1988.

First published in 2011

A catalogue record for this book is available from the British Library

ISBN: 978-1-78521-023-5

Published by Haynes Publishing, Sparkford, Yeovil,
Somerset BA22 7JJ, UK
Tel: 01963 442030 Fax: 01963 440001
Int. tel: +44 1963 442030 Int. fax: +44 1963 440001
E-mail: sales@haynes.co.uk
Website: www.haynes.co.uk

Haynes North America Inc., 861 Lawrence Drive,
Newbury Park, California 91320, USA

Images © Mirrorpix

Creative Director: Kevin Gardner
Designed for Haynes by BrainWave

Printed and bound in the US

When FOOTBALL *Was* FOOTBALL

WEST HAM

A Nostalgic Look at a Century of the Club

Iain Dale

Introduction

West Ham United. Those three words have meant so much to literally millions of people over the last 110 years. To many, following West Ham is a way of life, tantamount to a religion. Across the world it is a team that people both recognize and admire for what it has brought to the beautiful game over the decades. Mention West Ham anywhere in the world and the chances are that the person listening will smile and say "Bobby Moore". Because, as we all know, West Ham did in fact win the 1966 World Cup single-handedly. Bobby Moore was captain, Martin Peters scored and, as all remember so fondly, Geoff Hurst got the only hat-trick ever in a World Cup final. I was four years old at the time. My Dad tells me I watched the final with him. He taped it on a reel-to-reel tape recorder – sound only – and the tape still exists. Needless to say, I have absolutely no recollection of it.

I am slightly embarrassed to confess that I became a Hammer at the age of 10. It's not that I was embarrassed to become a Hammer, but it was the way it happened. Up to that point I had supported Manchester United. Well, it was natural – I lived in Essex! But they were relegated at the end of the 1971/2 season, and the shame of supporting a relegated side proved too much for an impressionable child of my tender years. My best friend, Roger Sizer, supported West Ham, and, being easily led, I decided to follow suit. It seemed a good idea at the time. Luckily, in my adult years I decided not to switch allegiances

each time West Ham were relegated.

This book is a unique collection of memorable and evocative photographs dating from the birth of the club right through to 1993, when the club resumed its proper place in the top flight of British football. Most of the photos are taken from the *Daily Mirror's* extensive archive and many are previously unpublished. From the early days through to the European glory days of the 1960s, from the FA Cup wins of 1975 and 1980 through to the unparalleled achievements of the "Boys of '86", this book is designed to take you through the entire history of Britain's most entertaining football club and bring to life many of the events, games and characters some newer fans may have not previously come across. Legends such as Syd Puddefoot, Bobby Moore and Billy Bonds are all pictured, along with scenes from many of the Hammers' most memorable games through the decades.

I hope that after reading this book you will have a greater understanding of the history of this great club and what makes it tick. This is the story of West Ham United, When Football Was Football, from the heart of the East End.

Iain Dale

Foreword by David Cross

On 8th December 1977 – my 27th birthday – I received the best present I am ever likely to receive. I signed for West Ham United. I arrived with some misgivings, wondering how I, a 6' 2" beanpole Lancastrian with a battering-ram reputation, was going to fit into a team with a history of cultured football and silky skilled footballers. A history that had been nurtured for over half a century.

I had been taught the rudiments of centre-forward play by Ron Saunders at Norwich City, had stood still for a couple of seasons at Coventry City but then been revitalized by a season under John Giles at West Bromwich Albion. Now I arrived at Upton Park hoping my next step would be an upward one.

I didn't know it then, but I had just signed for a manager who would become the biggest influence on my career. John Lyall improved my game to such an extent that he got me to the brink of the 1982 World Cup squad. But he also taught me about the history of the club, the ethos of the West Ham Academy and about the people who watched us.

The game was to be played with high quality football – with grace and style, as well as with pace and strength. He told me that the Upton Park fans would understand defeat but would never accept a lowering of the highest standards of football purism. They could understand a poor performance but never a lack of endeavour on the pitch.

He told me about the East End people – hard-working people, perhaps with a hard exterior, but, deep down, people with good hearts and a generosity of spirit. Some had survived the Blitz, some had gone through difficult times when the dockyards

David Cross playing against Spurs at White Hart Lane in September 1981, a game in which he scored all West Ham's four goals.

had shut down and had gone through financial downturns. They endured it all with fortitude and hope. They sang their song about the eternal optimist who sought good fortune but which always seemed to elude him, and when they walked up Green Street on a Saturday afternoon they knew what they wanted to see.

I was lucky. These people took me to their hearts and made my five seasons at Upton Park the happiest years of my footballing life. Despite playing for many other teams in my career West Ham is MY club. The first result I look for. The club I grew to love. My club.

This book is a book for the fans. I hope it brings back many happy memories of a time when football was a simple game, played by people like them.

David Cross

Iron Beginnings
1895-1900

The Thames Ironworks shipyard at Learmouth Wharf in Blackwall. It was here that Thames Ironworks FC was formed in 1895, the club that five years later became West Ham United.

The Founding of a Football Club

West Ham United was officially formed in 1900, but the club's forerunner was the Thames Ironworks, founded in June 1895 from the remnants of the Old Castle Swifts club, as announced in the *Thames Ironworks Gazette*. The founders were one of the shipbuilding company's foremen, David Taylor, who was a local football referee, and the owner of the company, Arnold Hills. Hills had a particularly enlightened attitude to employment and was well known for coming up with ideas to improve the lives of his employees. Initially playing as amateurs, the team featured several works' employees, including Walter Parks (clerk), Thomas Freeman (ships fireman), Tom Mundy, Walter Tranter and James Lindsay (all boiler-makers), William Chapman, George Sage, William Chamberlain and apprentice riveter Charlie Dove.

Thames Ironworks' first game took place on 7th September 1895 against the Woolwich-based Royal Ordnance Reserves. It was played on the ground of the by then defunct Castle Swifts at Hermit Road, Canning Town. The game ended in a 1-1 draw.

The team met some initial success, winning the inaugural West Ham Charity Cup against Barking after two replays in 1895 and the London League in 1897.

LEFT: Arnold Hills (1857-1927), Managing Director of Thames Ironworks.

RIGHT: Thames Ironworks team photo, 1896.

Claret & Blue

During their first four seasons the team played in dark blue shorts and shirts since the owner, Arnold Hills, had been a "blue" at Oxford University, but in 1897 they changed to sky blue shirts and white shorts. It was only at the start of the 1899 season that they adopted the current West Ham kit style of claret shirts with light blue sleeves and white shorts.

In June 1897 the club moved to a new stadium, financed by Arnold Hills, at the Memorial Grounds in East Ham. It cost £20,000 (£1 million in today's money) to build. Season tickets for the 1897/8 campaign were priced at 5 shillings (25p), with individual matches costing 4d admission (1½p).

At the start of the 1897/8 season, Arnold Hills wrote the following message to the team's players:

"To the players: – As an old footballer myself, I would say, get into good condition at the beginning of the season, keep on the ball, play an unselfish game, pay heed to your captain, and whatever the fortunes of the first half of the game, never despair of winning, and never give up doing your very best to the last minute of the match. That is the way to play football, and better still, that is the way to make yourselves men." (Quoted in *Iron in the Blood*)

In 1898 the club joined the Southern League Division Two and opened with a 3-0 victory away against Shepherd's Bush. The first league match at the Memorial Grounds was against Brentford, with the Ironsiders (as they were known) victorious by three goals to one. The season finished with Thames Ironworks topping the league, nine points ahead of Wolverton, their nearest rivals, winning promotion at their first attempt.

Thames Ironworks team photo, March 1898.

All Change

Season ticket prices doubled for the next season, which got off to a bad start with a 1-0 defeat away to Reading. The club was beset with problems on and off the pitch during this season, with the club secretary suspended for making illegal approaches to players from rival clubs, the team captain Harry Bradshaw dying on Boxing Day and a humiliating 7-0 defeat away to Tottenham Hotspur.

The first sign that all was not well with the ownership of Thames Ironworks came on 7th March 1900 when it was reported in the *West Ham Guardian* that: "It is announced that the committee of Thames Ironworks FC are to consider some sort of reorganisation. A proposal is evidently on the table. For one who has it on authority says it will 'if adopted, undoubtedly be to the club's advantage.' This is good news. Supporters are tired of seeing the club so low down as fourth from the bottom."

Owner Arnold Hills was having cashflow problems, having agreed to buy John Penn & Sons, and needed to raise funds. He knew he couldn't pump further money into a football club. Shortly before the season's end the *West Ham Guardian* reported that local people would be asked to buy 500 shares at £1 each, with Arnold Hills matching the sum. A few weeks later the West Ham Football Club Company Limited was formed. However, some shares remained unsold for several years. Thames Ironworks resigned from the Southern League and were wound up in June 1900. On 5th July, West Ham United Football Club was formally registered and were elected to the Southern League in Thames Ironworks' place. It may not have been the ending Arnold Hills had wished for, but there is little doubt that Mr Hills remains the great-grandfather of the club we know today.

Thames Ironworks team photo, 1899.

The Syd King Era
1900-1932

One game dominates the 32 years of Syd King's reign as West Ham's first manager – the FA Cup final of 1923. For a club that only joined the Football League four years earlier it was some achievement. The final itself wasn't memorable for the result – it is fondly remembered for the role played by a white horse called Billie.

The Early Years

West Ham United started their illustrious history in the Southern League, a league they remained in for the next 19 years until their election to League Division Two. Their first season started with a bang, with a 7-0 victory over Gravesend, with new signing Billy Grassam scoring four goals. Grassam finished as top scorer with 15 goals and the club ended up in a creditable sixth place. Off the field the club's finances remained precarious, with disappointing crowds and season tickets sales amounting to fewer than 200. By the end of the 1903/4 season, the club were verging on bankruptcy and only had the funds to pay one professional, Tommy Allison, over the summer.

The club's main benefactor, Arnold Hills, had also hit on hard times and was in no position to reduce the rent on the Memorial Grounds Stadium. Luckily, a local brewery stepped in and put up £20,000 to finance the building of a new stadium on the site of the Boleyn Castle playing fields off Green Street in East Ham. However, a further hitch occurred when the Home Office objected to a football club using the land, which was under the ownership of the Catholic Ecclesiastical Authorities. The new manager, Syd King, took it upon himself to see local Conservative MP Ernest Gray. Gray smoothed the path and the 1905/6 season opened at the Boleyn Ground with an emphatic 3-0 win against Millwall.

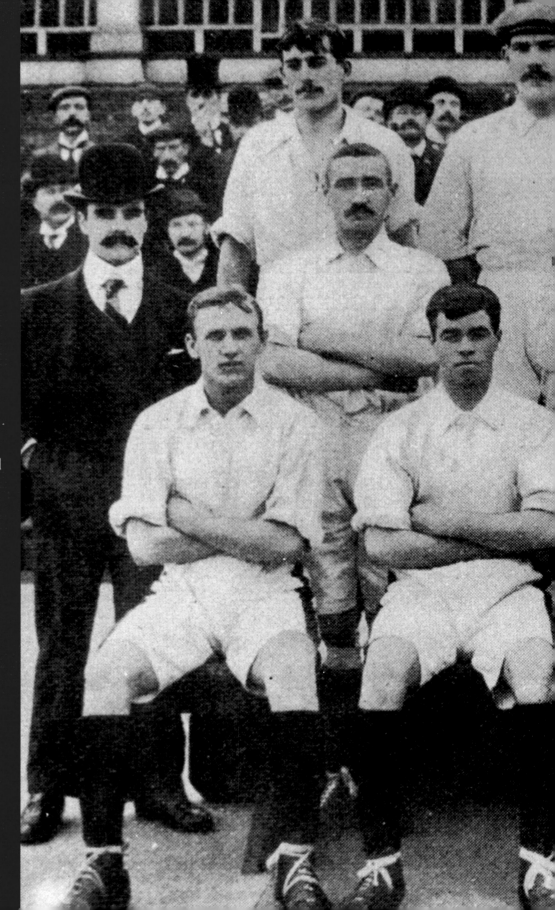

LEFT: West Ham Football Club team photo, 1900-1.

"It is the proud boast of the West Ham club that they turn out more local players than any other team in the South. The district has been described as a hot-bed of football and it is so. The raw material is found on the marshlands and open spaces round about; and after a season or so, the finished player leaves the East End workshop to better himself, as most ambitious young men will do. In the ranks of other organizations many old West Ham boys have distinguished themselves."

Association Football journal, 1905

West Ham team photo, 1904-5.

> *When training, Oxo is the only beverage used by our team and all speak if the supreme strength and power of endurance they have derived from its use.*
>
> Syd King reveals the team's chosen drink during the 1904/5 season.

–LEGENDS–

George Kitchen

George Kitchen was persuaded to join West Ham United from Everton by Syd King in 1905. Kitchen is seen as one of the outstanding goalkeepers of the time. His first match was against Swindon Town on 2nd September 1905. Kitchen scored the winning penalty and has gone down in history as the first goalkeeper to score on his debut. During the 1906/7 season the team only conceded 41 goals in 38 games. After playing for West Ham for six seasons, Kitchen was transferred to Southampton in 1912 and later retired from football to become a golf professional.

FOOTBALL –STATS–

George Kitchen

Name: George William Kitchen

Born: Fairfield, Derbyshire 1876

Died: Unknown

Position: Goalkeeper

West Ham Playing Career: 1905-12

Club Appearances: 205

Goals: 6

England Appearances: 0

Goals: 0

" *It won't make it easier for the goalkeeper; I should say that there will not be many penalty kicks stopped.*

Reacting in 1905 to the new rule that goalkeepers must remain under their crossbars when facing penalty kicks. "

Sack the Board... in 1908!

> *Frequently there were suspicions of favouritism in their choices.*
>
> The East Ham Echo explains why the directors handed over team selection to Syd King in 1908.

DIRECTORS.

J. W. Y. Cearns   J. Moss   G. C. Fundell, *Treas.*   H. Iggulden   W. White

E. S. King, *Sec.*
G. Handley

J. Grisdale, *Chairman.*
H. G. Sutton

H. Mattocks
T. Taylorson

RIGHT: West Ham United Football Club company directors, 1908-9.

–LEGENDS–

Danny Shea

The West Ham coach, Charlie Paynter, discovered Danny Shea in 1908 playing for the Builders' Arms pub team in Stratford. He soon signed him up to play for West Ham – and Shea was an instant success. As a skilful inside-forward Shea ended up the top goalscorer in his first season in the Southern League, with 20 goals to his name. This was followed by 31 goals in the next season, 28 goals in the 1910/11 season and 24 goals in the 1911/12 season. In 1913 Shea was transferred to Blackburn Rovers for the record fee of £2,000. Shea guested for West Ham during the war (while working as a docker) and briefly returned to Upton Park in 1920, but soon left for Fulham, eventually retiring from football in 1926 and becoming a publican. In his 290 appearances for the club he netted 186 goals.

> ## I punched both goals into the net in full view of several opponents.
>
> Shea admits to scoring two goals with his fist in a match shrouded in fog against Nottingham Forest in 1911.

BELOW: It is thought that this is a photo from a match against Millwall at the Den from around 1910 and that Danny Shea is the West Ham player in the foreground.

Scorecard:

1907-8	15-3
1908-9	41-20
1909-10	43-31
1910-11	39-28
1911-12	41-24
1912-13	22-15
1915-16	27-17
1916-17	32-32
1917-18	14-15
1920-21	16-1

FOOTBALL –STATS–

Danny Shea

Name: Daniel Harold Shea

Born: Wapping, 1887

Died: London, 1960

Position: Inside-forward

West Ham Playing Career: 1907-13, 1915-20

Club Appearances: 290

Goals: 186

England Appearances: 2

Goals: 0

The Lights Go Out Over Europe...

In the immediate pre-war years West Ham yo-yoed up and down the Southern League with a highest finish of third in 1912/13. They might have done better if they hadn't sold Danny Shea to League champions Blackburn halfway through the season. Shea was replaced by 19-year-old local boy Syd Puddefoot, who proved an immediate hit. But the club seemed to be on the up and there were high hopes of promotion from the Southern League the following season. War broke out, however, and West Ham players came under pressure to join up. Some did: the club only managed fourth place in 1913/14. Five West Ham players were killed in action – William Kennedy, Frank Cannon, Arthur Stallard, Fred Griffiths and William Jones. Key players George Hilsdon and Fred Harrison both suffered from gas attacks and never played for the club again.

LEFT: 7th November 1914: West Ham 0 Reading 0.

LEFT INSET: Tom Randall with the West Bromwich Albion captain before their second replay match on 2nd January 1913. West Ham went on to win the game 3-0.

23

The League Awaits

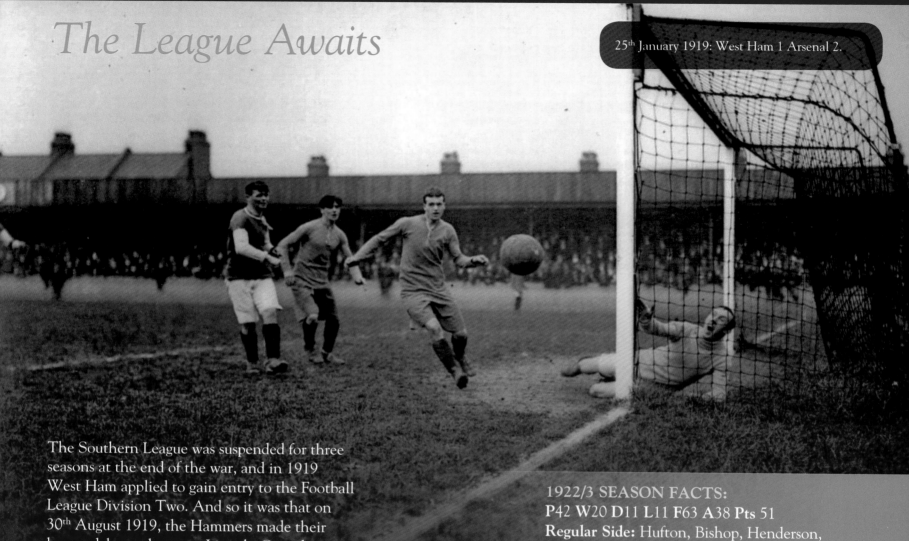

The Southern League was suspended for three seasons at the end of the war, and in 1919 West Ham applied to gain entry to the Football League Division Two. And so it was that on 30th August 1919, the Hammers made their league debut at home to Lincoln City, drawing 1-1. The second match proved to be a disaster, with Barnsley beating the league new boys 7-0. But West Ham gradually found their feet and finished seventh. The next season was even better, with the Hammers climbing to fifth, with Syd Puddefoot scoring 29 goals in 38 games. The following season saw a one place improvement with Vic Watson taking over goalscoring responsibilities from Syd Puddefoot, who had controversially been sold to Falkirk. But it was the 1922/3 season that proved to be hugely successful, bringing promotion to the top flight and a first-ever FA Cup final appearance.

1922/3 SEASON FACTS:
P42 W20 D11 L11 F63 A38 Pts 51
Regular Side: Hufton, Bishop, Henderson, Kay, Richards, Young, Brown, Moore, Ruffell, Tresarden, Watson.
Top Scorers: Watson 22, Moore 15
Captain: George Kay

" *Joy at West Ham as news was received that the club's application to join the Football League was successful.*

Athletic News, 1919 "

–LEGENDS–

Syd Puddefoot

In 1912 Syd Puddefoot was signed by West Ham manager Syd King after he saw him playing for the London Juniors. Puddefoot, a centre-forward, joined a strong team with two outstanding strikers. However, Puddefoot soon proved his worth, scoring his debut goal on 21st March 1913 against Brighton & Hove Albion, and in the 10 subsequent games he found the net 12 times. He went on to set an FA Cup goalscoring record for West Ham on 10th January 1914, scoring five times in an 8-1 victory over Chesterfield. Puddefoot was much loved by the fans and it nearly caused a riot when Syd King sold him to Falkirk for the British record fee of £5,000 in February 1922. Puddefoot returned to his boyhood club in 1931, aged 37, in an ill-fated attempt to stop West Ham from being relegated from the First Division. When Puddefoot retired in 1933 he had scored 207 goals in his 308 appearances for West Ham.

Scorecard:

Season	
1912-13	4-1
1913-14	20-16
1914-15	37-18
1915-16	31-25
1916-17	34-24
1917-18	35-35
1918-19	14-16
1919-20	43-26
1920-21	39-29
1921-22	29-14
1931-32	7-0
1932-33	15-3

> *I most sincerely think Syd Puddefoot is the best centre-forward the world has ever seen.*
>
> Charlie Payner, speaking in 1922.

FOOTBALL –STATS–

Syd Puddefoot

Name: Sydney Charles Puddefoot

Born: Bow, 1894

Died: Rochford, 1972

Position: Centre-forward

West Ham Playing Career: 1912-22, 1931-33

Club Appearances: 308

Goals: 207

England Appearances: 2

Goals: 0

Winning Promotion

The 1922/3 season started off with very high hopes but with only two victories in their first 10 games, the Hammers languished in 17th place. It was only after a 3-1 away win over Coventry City at the end of December that West Ham finally sparked into life, commencing an unbeaten run of 23 games. Vic Watson and William Moore scored 37 goals between them. But it was West Ham's away form that made the difference: they won 11 games away from home but only 9 at Upton Park. Indeed, 42 goals were scored during their travels, exactly double the number scored at home. West Ham ended the season on 51 points in second place, only winning promotion thanks to a superior goal average to Leicester City.

THE F.A. CUP FINAL — WEST HAM FOOTBALL TEAM.

Mr KING (SECRETARY)   W. HENDERSON   S. BISHOP   G. KAY   A.E. HUFTON   J. YOUNG   J. TRESADERN   C. PAYNTER (TRAINER)

R. RICHARDS   W. BROWN   V. WATSON   W. MOORE   J. RUFFELL

I'm forever blowing bubbles, pretty bubbles in the air.

West Ham's team anthem was first heard in the 1920s, sung in praise of Billy "Bubbles" Murray. It originally comes from the musical 'The Passing Show of 1918'.

ABOVE: 1923 FA Cup final team.

–LEGENDS– George Kay

George Kay joined West Ham for a fee of £100 in 1919, making his debut against Barnsley on 8th September 1919. Kay was a well respected member of the team and in 1922 Syd King made him captain. He captained the West Ham team when they reached the final of the 1923 FA Cup, played at the newly built Wembley Stadium. Kay went on to become the first West Ham player to play more than 200 league games for the club. He finally left West Ham in 1926, mainly for health reasons. He went on to manage Luton, Southampton and Liverpool, winning the first post-war Football League Championship in 1946/7. He was afflicted by poor health in later life and retired from football management in 1951, passing away only three years later, at the age of 62.

FOOTBALL –STATS–

George Kay

Name: George Kay

Born: Manchester, 21st September 1891

Died: Liverpool, 18th April 1954

Position: Centre-half

West Ham Playing Career: 1919-26

Club Appearances: 282

Goals: 22

England Appearances: 0

Goals: 0

The Road to Wembley

West Ham's first-ever FA Cup final took place before the end of the season and before West Ham's promotion to the top flight was confirmed. Despite needing two replays on the way to the final, West Ham had managed to avoid meeting any First Division sides. Hull, Brighton, Plymouth and Southampton were all despatched before a tricky semi-final meeting away to Derby. It proved to be a memorable day, with West Ham triumphing 5-2.

First round	13th January	A	Hull City	3-2	Watson 2, Moore
Second round	3rd February	A	Brighton	1-1	Watson
Second round replay	7th February	H	Brighton	1-0	Moore
Third round	24th February	H	Plymouth Argyle	2-0	Moore, Richards
Fourth round	10th March	A	Southampton	1-1	Watson
Fourth round replay	14th March	H	Southampton	1-1	Watson
Fourth round replay	19th March	Villa Park	Southampton	1-0	Brown
Semi-final	24th March	Stamford Bridge	Derby County	5-2	Brown 2, Moore 2, Ruffell
Final	28th April	Wembley	Bolton Wanderers	0-2	

The first match under the twin towers proved memorable not for the game itself but for the size of the crowd, which was estimated at 200,000, although the official attendance was 126,047. The pitch had to be cleared before the kick-off with the help of a white horse called Billie. The match was less memorable, with Bolton running out 2-0 winners, but West Ham were finally on the football map. Despite another semi-final appearance four years later, it was, though, to be another 41 years before West Ham would grace the Wembley pitch again.

MATCH STATS – FA CUP FINAL 1923
Date & Venue: 28th April 1923 at
Wembley Stadium
Bolton Wanderers 2(1) West Ham United 0(0)
Bolton: Pym, Haworth, Finney, Nuttall, Seddon,
Jennings, Butler, Jack, J R Smith, J Smith, Vizard
West Ham: Hufton, Henderson, Young, Bishop,
Kay, Tresadern, Richards, Brown, Watson,
Moore, Ruffell
Goals: Jack (2m), J R Smith (53m)
Attendance: 126,047
Captain: George Kay
Manager: Syd King

THE DAILY MIRROR, April 30, 1923.

Squeak Plays Cricket: See Page 11

The Daily Mirror

NET SALE MUCH THE LARGEST OF ANY DAILY PICTURE NEWSPAPER

Turn to page 11 and— —enjoy a hearty laugh.

F.A. CUP FINAL PHOTOGRAPHS: SCENES ON AND AROUND THE FIELD OF PLAY

The rival captains shaking hands before the start of play.

Butler putting the ball through for Bolton only to be given offside. Note crowd on goal line.

Moore, of West Ham, taking a pass from Ruffell.

Bolton appeal as West Ham get away with the ball.

The King (on right) presenting the medals. Smith, with the Cup, on left.

A West Ham back effecting an energetic clearance.

The King, accompanied by the Duke of Devonshire, gazing on the amazing scene.

Red Cross men attending to one of the many people injured.

A mascot cup for Bolton's charabanc.

Despite the peculiar circumstances of the Wembley Cup Final, the match, when once a start was possible, produced interesting and clever play. The presence of the crowd on the touch-lines considerably hampered the work of the wingers, but both teams gave good displays of effective combination and determined defence.

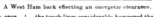

Printed and Published by THE DAILY MIRROR NEWSPAPERS, LTD., 23-29, Bouverie-street, London, E.C.4.—Monday, April 30, 1923. Telephone Central 5440.

BRITISH EMPIRE EXHIBITION (1924)

PROGRAMME & SOUVENIR FINAL TIE

OF THE FOOTBALL ASSOCIATION'S ENGLISH CUP COMPETITION

To be played at

THE EMPIRE STADIUM WEMBLEY

April 28th 1923

BOLTON WANDERERS
v
WEST HAM UNITED

PRICE THREEPENCE

ABOVE: 1923 FA Cup final programme.

LEFT AND RIGHT: Newspaper coverage, 28th May 1923.

The Daily Mirror 24 PAGES

NET SALE MUCH THE LARGEST OF ANY DAILY PICTURE NEWSPAPER

No. 6,079.   Registered at the G.P.O. as a Newspaper.   MONDAY, APRIL 30, 1923   One Penny.

POLICE v. CROWD: WEMBLEY'S FIRST CUP FINAL

A remarkable photograph, taken from the air, of the Stadium at Wembley, with spectators swarming over the playing pitch, while bands are clustered outside.

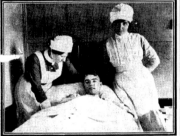

Arnold Ratcliffe, of Bolton. He was crushed and picked up unconscious.

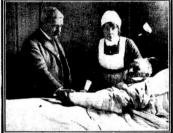

Thomas McGregor, of Islington, in hospital with a broken arm and leg.

Official records will claim that the first contest to be staged at the Empire Stadium, Wembley, was the final for the Football Association Challenge Cup between West Ham United and Bolton Wanderers. The many thousands who journeyed to Wembley on Saturday will, however, long retain the memory of an earlier struggle in which the opposing elements were police and public, the ultimate victory resting with the force whose untiring efforts eventually produced order from utter chaos.

"Should auld acquaintance be forgot"

Signatures

Souvenir of

BANQUET

held on
Saturday, December 8th, 1923
at
ABERCORN ROOMS
GE HOTEL   LONDON

To commemorate the participation of the
BOLTON WANDERERS & WEST HAM
UNITED FOOTBALL CLUBS in the
FINAL TIE of the FOOTBALL ASSOCIATION
CUP at WEMBLEY on APRIL 28th, 1923

Chairman - THOS. H. KIRKUP, Esq.

Tramtastic

BELOW: Decorated tram to celebrate the Hammers getting to the final.

> I am too disappointed to talk. I haven't got over it yet. I want to forget it.
>
> Syd King reacting to the Cup final defeat.

–LEGENDS– Jimmy Ruffell

Jimmy Ruffell was signed by Syd King for West Ham in March 1920 and made his debut in September 1921 in a 3-0 victory against Port Vale. Ruffell played at outside-left and went on to make 548 appearances for the Hammers, a record that wasn't beaten until Bobby Moore surpassed it in 1973. Ruffell is one of West Ham's greatest ever wingers, netting 166 cup and league goals in his time at the club and was the top goalscorer in both the 1927/8 and 1934/5 seasons. He was part of the great team that contested the first FA Cup final at Wembley, and also had six caps for England under his belt. Ruffell left West Ham in 1937 and finally retired from football in 1938. He will always be considered a true Hammers legend.

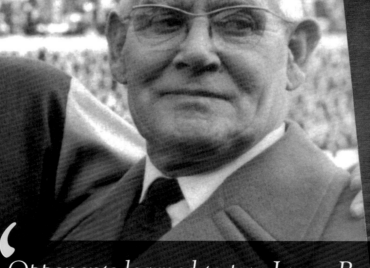

Bobby Moore & Jimmy Ruffell in 1974.

Scorecard:

Season	Apps-Goals
1921-22	15-0
1922-23	42-7
1923-24	42-2
1924-25	48-12
1925-26	41-12
1926-27	40-14
1927-28	41-19
1928-29	42-20
1929-30	44-13
1930-31	38-13
1931-32	41-15
1932-33	8-0
1933-34	24-8
1934-35	38-20
1935-36	32-11
1936-37	12-0

" *Opponents learned to pay James Ruffell the compliment of close marking; it was fatal to give him full rein to his exceptional speed and flashing shots.* "

A Century of International Football

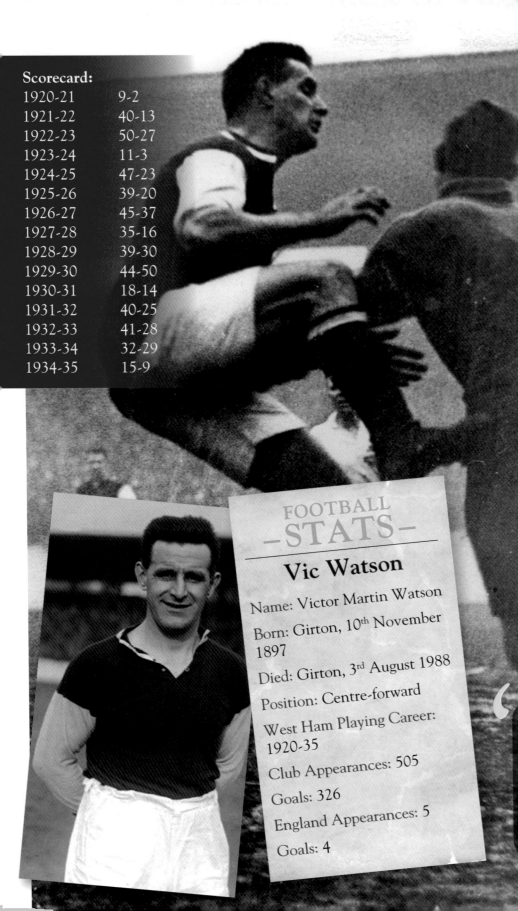

Scorecard:

Season	Record
1920-21	9-2
1921-22	40-13
1922-23	50-27
1923-24	11-3
1924-25	47-23
1925-26	39-20
1926-27	45-37
1927-28	35-16
1928-29	39-30
1929-30	44-50
1930-31	18-14
1931-32	40-25
1932-33	41-28
1933-34	32-29
1934-35	15-9

FOOTBALL —STATS—

Vic Watson

Name: Victor Martin Watson

Born: Girton, 10th November 1897

Died: Girton, 3rd August 1988

Position: Centre-forward

West Ham Playing Career: 1920-35

Club Appearances: 505

Goals: 326

England Appearances: 5

Goals: 4

Vic Watson

Vic Watson was a talented centre-forward and joined West Ham in March 1920 for the transfer fee of £50 from Wellingborough as cover for Hammers hero Syd Puddefoot. When Puddefoot was sold to Falkirk in 1922, Watson took his place as centre-forward. Watson scored 27 league and cup goals during the 1922/3 season, playing a huge part in West Ham's promotion to the First Division that year. Disaster struck in 1923 when Watson broke his toe during the first match of the season, which left him out of the side until April 1924. Vic Watson is considered by many to be the greatest centre-forward the club has ever seen. During his 15 years at the club he made 505 appearances, netting 326 goals, including 13 hat-tricks – a club record that is unlikely ever to be beaten in the modern era. His finest hour came on 29th February 1929 when he scored a double hat-trick in the 8-2 thumping of Leeds United at Upton Park. In 1935 he left for Southampton, where he spent one season before retiring.

> *Dashing centre-forward whose tactic was to persistently harass the opposing defence.*
>
> Football writer

The Roaring Twenties

West Ham's debut in the top flight of English football was nothing if not steady. They finished 13th in both of their first two seasons. In the 1925/6 season some terrible away form, with only one away win throughout the season, saw them slump to 18th. The next season proved to be the club's best ever, with Vic Watson scoring 34 goals in 42 games, but this time it was home form which let the side down, with only nine wins at the Boleyn Ground all season. In contrast there were 10 away victories. In each of the following two seasons the Hammers finished 17th, with Vic Watson and Jimmy Ruffell again proving consistent goalscorers. In 1929/30 Vic Watson achieved the astonishing feat of scoring 42 goals in 40 games, which was the key to them finishing in seventh place. But the yo-yo plumbed the depths again in the following two seasons and at the end of the 1931/2 season the Hammers finished bottom and were relegated to Division Two, after they lost all of their last seven games despite the return to West Ham of the legendary Syd Puddefoot. If they had drawn one and won one of those seven games they would have retained their top flight status, but it wasn't to be.

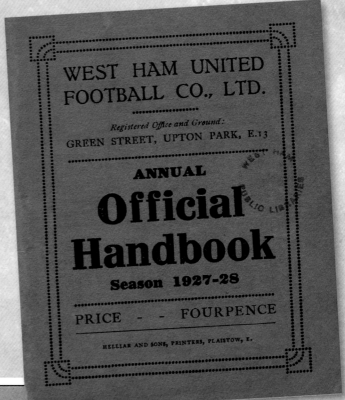

WEST HAM UNITED FOOTBALL CO., LTD.

Registered Office and Ground:
GREEN STREET, UPTON PARK, E.13

ANNUAL

Official Handbook

Season 1927-28

PRICE - - FOURPENCE

HELLIAR AND SONS, PRINTERS, PLAISTOW, E.

LEFT: H. M. the King of Denmark makes Jack Hebden smile at half-time of a friendly played in Denmark on 15th May 1927. West Ham won all five matches of their post-season Scandinavian Tour.

> *West Ham went out of the First Division in an inglorious manner at Stamford Bridge… It was hard to realise from this exhibition that this was one of the most vital matches in the history of the club.*
>
> Football writer Charles Buchan on West Ham's exit from the top flight in 1932.

ABOVE: West Ham team photo, 1928/9.

RIGHT: *Daily Mirror* golf competition for footballers, April 1924. Bill Williams (West Ham), Tommy Clay (Spurs), Tommy Hampson (West Ham), Edward Wallington (Arsenal).

–LEGENDS–

Ted Hufton

Ted Hufton joined West Ham in 1915 for £350 from Sheffield United, and became the Club's regular goalkeeper in 1919 after the Hammers goalkeeper Joe Hughes said to Syd King that Hufton was a "better goalie than I'll ever be". In his first two seasons Hufton saved 11 out of 18 penalty kicks, and in the 1920/1 season Hufton did not concede more than two goals in the 38 games he played in – the best goals-against record in the country that year. He was part of the West Ham team that went on to win promotion in the 1922/3 season, and appeared at the White Horse final at the newly built Wembley Stadium. Hufton made 456 appearances for the Hammers during his 17 years at West Ham, ranking him 12th on the list of loyal servants to the club. After the Second World War he returned to Upton Park as press room steward on match days.

> " Ted Hufton, the greatest goalie ever.
>
> Ernie Gregory "

> " Ted Hufton, the goalkeeper, was another of my heroes, and he was always in the Press Room after a match at Upton Park, dispensing yarns and memories with the utmost amiability.
>
> Ted Fenton "

FOOTBALL –STATS–

Ted Hufton

Name: Arthur Edward Hufton

Born: Southwell, Notts, 25th November 1892

Died: Swansea, 2nd February 1967

Position: Goalkeeper

West Ham Playing Career: 1915-32

Club Appearances: 456

Goals: 0

England Appearances: 6

Goals: 0

The Life and Death of Syd King

"West Ham is Syd King" said the *East End Echo* in its 1923 Cup final issue. Indeed, King was master of all he surveyed. He finished playing at the end of the 1901/2 season and then took over as club secretary and manager, a position he was to hold for the next 30 years. He had the complete trust of the Board, he controlled all transfers and effectively ran the club on a day-to-day basis. "Flamboyance" should have been his middle name. He personified the very meaning of the phrase "colourful character". In 1931 he was given shares in the club, but only 18 months later he was relieved of his duties. A Board meeting minute from 7th November 1932 recorded: "It was unanimously decided that until further notice C. Paynter be given sole control of players and that E.S. King be notified accordingly." This came about because of King's persistent state of drunkenness, insubordination and questionable business dealings. Two months later he committed suicide. It was a very sad end for a proud man, who had much to be proud of.

The Charlie Paynter Era
1932-1950

West Ham team photo, 1935. Charlie Paynter is on the immediate left.

With the Syd King era closing and relegation beckoning, the club turned to long time servant Charlie Paynter to revive the Hammers' fortunes. He was to remain at the helm for 18 years, during which time the Hammers struggled to regain their former glories. It was to be a quarter of a century before West Ham would grace the First Division again. Indeed, in their first season back in Division Two West Ham were very nearly relegated to the Third Division, finishing in 20th place, one point ahead of relegated Chesterfield, despite another 24 goals from the ever prolific Vic Watson.

Vic Watson and Dixie Dean kick off the 1933 FA Cup semi-final against Everton. Everton progressed to the final after a 2-1 win.

Two years after that West Ham narrowly missed out on a return to Division One, finishing in third place, one point behind Bolton. The following season a victory against local rivals Charlton at the end of the season and another victory in their final game away at Sheffield United would also have resulted in promotion – both were lost.

Club Director A C Davis got himself into hot water with some ill-chosen words after the Charlton game in which he appeared to say that the Board would prefer to be playing at the top of the Second Division rather than the bottom of the first. The Board issued a strongly worded statement denying this was their view, but having sold leading scorer Dave Mangnall (23 goals in 25 games) midway through the season it was easy to see why people feared the worst.

The final three seasons before the outbreak of the Second World War were unmemorable with finishes of 6th, 9th and 11th.

ABOVE: Left to right: Wood, Deacon, Mills, Wilson and Morton.

LEFT: Vic Watson and Joe Musgrave, 1933.

–LEGENDS–

Len Goulden

Len Goulden was a Charlie Paynter discovery. He signed schoolboy forms in 1931 and gained initial footballing experience by being loaned out to Chelmsford City and Leyton Orient. He immediately formed a storming partnership with Jimmy Ruffell. The Second World War interrupted his career but he was a key member of the West Ham team that won the 1940 War Cup. After the war he was transferred to Chelsea for £4,500, scoring 17 goals in 111 appearances before retiring in 1950. He won 14 caps for England and played in the famous England international against Germany in 1938 when the England team were forced to give the Nazi salute. When he scored off the crossbar he reportedly screamed "Let 'em salute that one". In 1952 he was appointed manager of Watford, a position he held for four years.

Scorecard:

1932-33	7-1
1933-34	42-8
1934-35	42-3
1935-36	40-15
1936-37	44-15
1937-38	36-9
1938-39	42-4

FOOTBALL –STATS–

Len Goulden

Name: Leonard Arthur Goulden

Born: Hackney, 16th July 1912

Died: Cornwall, 14th February 1995

Position: Inside-left

West Ham Playing Career: 1933-39

Club Appearances: 253

Goals: 55

England Appearances: 14

Goals: 4

Len Goulden (right) posing with team-mate Jackie Morton.

> "Len met the ball on the run; without surrendering any pace, his left leg cocked back like the trigger of a gun, snapped forward and he met the ball full face on the volley. To use modern parlance, his shot was like an Exocet missile. The German goalkeeper may well have seen it coming, but he could do absolutely nothing about it. From 25 yards the ball screamed into the roof of the net with such power that the netting was ripped from two of the pegs by which it was tied to the crossbar. It was the greatest goal I ever saw in football."
>
> Sir Stanley Matthews describing Len Goulden's goal against Germany.

WEST HAM UNITED FOOTBALL CO., LTD

Boleyn Ground, Green Street, Upton Park, E.13

West Ham United v. Norwich City

FOOTBALL LEAGUE REGIONAL COMPETITION

Christmas Day, 25th December, 1939   Kick-off 11.0 p.m

WEST HAM UNITED 4
Colours : Claret and Blue

RIGHT   LEFT

1 Cann

2 Bicknell   3 Chalkley

4 Fenton   5 Walker, R   6 Barrett

7 Foxall   8 Curtis   9 Foreman   10 Goulden   11 Wood

Referee : Mr. A. J. GIBBONS

Linesmen : Messrs. F. S. C. RIGGS (Red Stripe Flag) and O. W. CURTIS (Blue Stripe Flag)

11 Furness   10 Manders   9 Chadwick   8 Acquroff   7 Plunkett

6 Proctor   5 Reilly   4 Robinson

3 Taylor   2 Dale

1 Burns

LEFT   **NORWICH CITY 1**   RIGHT

First of all let us wish you all a happy Xmas and the brightest and most prosperous of New Years. Associated with these wishes are directors, officials and players still at Upton Park and players in the Services who, though away, wish to be remembered to the Hammers' fans with whom they have spent so many happy hours.

Optimism is one of the characteristics of player and spectator alike. Who knows? 1940—41 may find us back in the piping times of Peace and in the throes of promotion and relegation struggles and F.A. Cup-ties.

OUR VISITORS

Norwich are to-day's welcome guests and we look forward to a game worthy of Xmas morning traditions. We suffered defeat at Norwich in our first encounter of this competition, but we anticipate that the Canaries will find to-day's match a more difficult matter. However, all we ask is a keen, sporting 90 minutes, chock full of first class soccer, and we shall not quarrel over the result.

In normal times we should be asking you to "close up" so as to enable all fans to get into the ground.

Now, we feel inclined to ask you to "spread out" in order to delude ourselves that we have a "Full House."

LAST SATURDAY WEEK'S GAME

Last Saturday week's game was great. Not because we won so handsomely but rather for the reason that both elevens put up such good exhibitions of all that make this game attractive, and despite the fact that our score might easily have gone into double figures the Orient emerged as having contributed every bit as much to our enjoyment as the Hammers.

Again our thanks go to Fulham and Arsenal and Harry Cann and George Curtis for their assistance.

LAST SATURDAY'S GAME

The result of Saturday's game v. Crystal Palace was a true indication of the match. Both elevens played exhilarating soccer which was a treat to watch.

TO-MORROW

To-morrow we shall be away to the 'Spurs. No
continued overleaf

Wartime West Ham

A roof spotter looks out for signs of an air raid while West Ham play Chelsea in December 1940.

"

West Ham will commence the season under ground difficulties.

The Stratford Express censors get round admitting that the Boleyn Ground had been bombed in 1944.

"

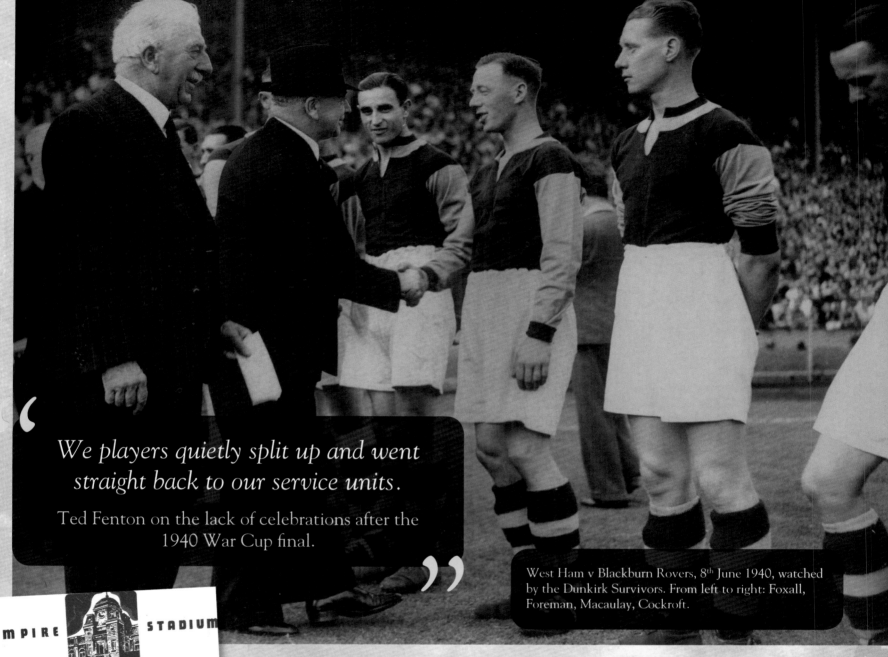

> *We players quietly split up and went straight back to our service units.*
>
> Ted Fenton on the lack of celebrations after the 1940 War Cup final.

West Ham v Blackburn Rovers, 8th June 1940, watched by the Dunkirk Survivors. From left to right: Foxall, Foreman, Macaulay, Cockroft.

EMPIRE STADIUM

WEMBLEY

THE FOOTBALL LEAGUE
WAR
CUP FINAL

BLACKBURN ROVERS
V
WEST HAM UNITED

SATURDAY, JUNE 8TH, 1940

OFFICIAL PROGRAMME • SIXPENCE

West Ham's 1939/40 campaign lasted only three matches before the outbreak of the Second World War brought league football to a shuddering halt. Having been tipped for promotion, it was no surprise that the Hammers reached the first Football League War Cup final against Blackburn Rovers, beating Chelsea, Leicester, Huddersfield, Birmingham and Fulham along the way. The final took place at 6.30pm on 8th June 1940. Sam Small scored in the 34th minute to give West Ham a 1-0 win.

During the war West Ham played in the Regional League South but the quality of the football was variable with nearly 40 different players being used each season. In August 1944 a V-1 flying bomb fell on the Boleyn Ground, which led to West Ham having to play all their matches away for the first four months of the season.

When proper league football resumed in August 1946 West Ham's first team contained only three players from the pre-war era – Charlie Bicknell, Harry Medhurst and Dick Walker. The immediate post-war years proved a bit of a let-down, with finishes of 12th, 6th and 7th. But it was the 1949/50 season that proved disastrous, with West Ham just managing to avoid a bottom two finish. Promotion back to Division One seemed a long way off.

It was at this point that Charlie Paynter decided to retire and former player Ted Fenton was appointed in his stead. Paynter had clocked up 50 years' service with West Ham as coach, club secretary and then manager. It was a remarkable record, and one which the club rewarded with a testimonial.

–LEGENDS–

Jackie Morton

Jackie Morton joined West Ham in 1931 after being signed from Gainsborough for £600, and made his debut against Arsenal in March 1932. He was the club's automatic choice on the left wing for the next seven years. Morton made 275 appearances and netted 57 goals during his time with the Hammers. When the Second World War broke out Morton retired from football and never returned. He is fondly remembered for becoming a bookmaker in his later years.

FOOTBALL –STATS–

Jackie Morton

Name: John Morton

Born: Sheffield, 26th February 1914

Died: 8th March 1986

Position: Forward

West Ham Playing Career: 1932-39

Club Appearances: 275

Goals: 57

England Appearances: 1

Goals: 1

Scorecard:

Season	Score
1931-32	5-1
1932-33	42-13
1933-34	44-6
1934-35	42-7
1935-36	26-5
1936-37	41-14
1937-38	40-3
1938-39	35-8

> " *Frail looking winger. Fast, possessed a multitude of tricks and a good shot.* "

FOOTBALL
–STATS–

Ernie Gregory

Name: Ernie Gregory

Born: Stratford, 10th November 1921

Position: Goalkeeper

West Ham Playing Career: 1939-59

Club Appearances: 481

England Appearances: 0

Goals: 0

Ernie Gregory

Ernie Gregory was spotted by Charlie Paynter when he played for West Ham Boys against Preston Boys at the final of the English Boys Trophy at Upton Park. Gregory signed for West Ham in 1936 and finally made his debut in 1939. During the Second World War he managed to find time to play 60 games for his club. In the 1947/8 season he was ever present, but unfortunately was ruled out during the next season following an injury. Gregory was famed for his often colourful language during a match. He finally retired at the age of 38 after making 481 appearances for the Hammers, 382 of them in the league. He went on to coach the reserves, and then the first team, and helped with team administration. He finally left the club in May 1987, after a 51-year association with the Irons.

Goalkeeper Gregory dives too late as Perry scores Blackpool's second goal.

> " He gave the impression of solid imperturbability, although anyone standing close enough to the West Ham goal might have heard some rather colourful language. "
>
> Charles Korr

The Ted Fenton Era
1950-1961

> *The only way to build the club was youth. There were lots of good players around, but I had no money to buy the key players we needed. There was always the problems of running a club on a shoe-string.*
>
> Ted Fenton

At coach door Johnny Dick; below him Andy Malcolm, then, left to right: Harry Obeney, Joe Kirkup, Malcolm Musgrove, Noel Cantwell, John Bond, Ken Brown and Noel Dwyer.

Birth of the Academy

Ted Fenton can truly lay claim to starting the Academy of Football. It was he who, knowing that the club was never likely to provide huge transfer resources, put in place the youth development policy that was to reap such dividends in the coming decades. And so he began to build the side that would eventually gain promotion later in the decade. His first few seasons in charge were less than notable, with finishes of 13th, 12th, 14th, 13th, 8th, 16th and 8th. Perhaps the most interesting element was the advent of floodlit football at the Boleyn.

FOOTBALL – STATS –

Ted Fenton

Name: Edward Fenton

Born: Forest Gate, 7th November 1914

Died: Peterborough, 12th July 1992

Position: Wing-half

West Ham Playing Career: 1932-46

Club Appearances: 163

Goals: 27

West Ham Managerial Career: Assistant Manager 1948-50, Manager 1950-61

"We were the first team to eat steak before meals... We were told to put a ball between two players and you take two players out. John Bond and Noel Cantwell were the first of the overlapping full-backs... We used to train at Forest Gate skating rink – it was narrow, so you could practise working in tight situations."

Ernie Gregory

ABOVE: West Ham 5 Sheffield 1 – 19th January 1952.

RIGHT: West Ham v Swansea – 15th November 1952. West Ham striker attempting a header on the Swansea goal at Upton Park. The final score was a 3-0 victory to the Hammers.

BELOW: West Ham team photo, 1951.

–LEGENDS–

Malcolm Allison

Ted Fenton signed Malcolm Allison for £7,000 in February 1951. Fenton made his debut playing centre-half against Chesterfield on 7th March 1951. The next season Allison replaced Dick Walker as captain of West Ham, but he had a turbulent relationship with Fenton that clearly affected the attitudes of the players, as demonstrated by a series of poor end-of-season finishes. Allison eventually took over the coaching of the club and implemented a controlled training regime, and also acted as a mentor to the younger players, especially future World Cup captain Bobby Moore. In 1958 Allison's playing career was suddenly cut short after he had his lung removed as a result of tuberculosis. Big Mal will always be remembered as one of English football's most flamboyant and intriguing characters.

> *You're not a real manager unless you've been sacked.*
>
> Malcolm Allison

> *Malcolm Allison was a strong man… He battled for what he wanted… He had an open-mindedness to try things. He had the same enthusiasm as Johnny Bond and Noel Cantwell, they were people who were progressive about their football.*
>
> John Lyall

FOOTBALL –STATS–

Malcolm Allison

Name: Malcolm Alexander Allison

Born: Dartford, 5th September 1927

Died: 14th October 2010

Position: Centre-half

West Ham Playing Career: 1951-57

Club Appearances: 258

Goals: 10

England Appearances: 0

Goals: 0

–LEGENDS–

John Bond

John Bond joined West Ham from the Colchester Casuals in March 1950, but he wouldn't go on to make his league debut until two seasons later. Bond had the ability to score goals as a right-back and as a result he remained a regular in the Hammers team. His partnership with Noel Cantwell also proved particularly useful in netting goals. During the 1957/8 season, Bond only missed one game and scored eight goals and was also a member of the line-up that won the 1964 FA Cup final. After 16 years at the club Bond was transferred to Torquay. In his time he made 444 appearances and netted 37 goals.

> " When I left West Ham to go off and coach, Ron told me all I needed was a good memory. He said: 'If you remember all the things we've done together, you'll be all right'. "
>
> John Bond

FOOTBALL –STATS–

John Bond

Name: John Frederick Bond

Born: Dedham, 17th December 1932

Position: Right-back

West Ham Playing Career: 1950-66

Club Appearances: 444

Goals: 37

England Appearances: 0

Goals: 0

The Academy of Football

When Ted Fenton became West Ham manager in 1950 he knew he wouldn't be able to pay huge transfer fees to sign the players the club needed. Instead, he looked to the long term, and instituted a youth policy that was to reap dividends for decades to come. 1958 proved to be a notable year, not just because West Ham had returned to the top flight of British football, but for the debut of a youngster who would go on to be one of the world's greatest players. His name? Bobby Moore.

"I'd been a professional for two and a half months and Malcolm had taught me everything I know… When Malcolm was coaching schoolboys he took a liking to me when I don't think anyone else at West Ham saw anything special in me… I looked up to the man. It's not too strong to say I loved him.

Bobby Moore

Few could have foretold the impact the young defender would have not just on West Ham, but on world football. First off the production line was Moore's debut in a memorable home game against Manchester United in early September. A 3-2 victory propelled the Hammers to the top of the league. Moore would only appear in four more games that season, but his promise was clear for all to see.

FAR LEFT: West Ham training, February 1958.

LEFT: Training in August 1958.

BELOW: A young Bobby Moore (centre) with Andy Smillie (left) and Tony Scott (right).

"
The selection of Bobby Moore at left-half proved justified by a display which foreshadows a grand future for a 17-year-old called upon to make his debut against one of Europe's leading sides.

A review of Bobby Moore's debut against Manchester United in the West Ham match day programme.
"

In the 1958/9 season West Ham finished at the dizzy heights of sixth, largely due to star striker John Dick's 27 goals in 41 games and Vic Keeble's 20 goals in 32. It wasn't until almost 30 years later that the Hammers boasted such a prolific partnership. The initial success in Division One was not to be repeated for some time. Things weren't helped when Ted Fenton suddenly resigned as manager in March 1961 in circumstances that have still not been explained half a century later. For the first time, West Ham looked beyond the confines of Upton Park for a successor. He came from Arsenal: Ron Greenwood.

Arsenal 1, West Ham 2, March 1959.

Action during a 6-1 drubbing at Old Trafford in September 1960.

ABOVE: West Ham v Manchester United – 16 April 1960. Harry Gregg ends up in the goal after Musgrove scores the Hammers' first goal in a 2-1 win.

BELOW: Welsh wizard Phil Woosnam, later to run the North American Soccer League, played 138 league games for West Ham between 1958 and 1962, scoring 26 goals.

Child supporters at Upton Park, 9th April 1959.

The Ron Greenwood Era
1961-1974

Simply Greenwood

The 1961 season saw the advent of the Ron Greenwood era. It also saw the north bank of the Boleyn Ground roofed for the first time and a new set of more powerful floodlights installed. Greenwood was determined to reshape the team and started to introduce younger players like Geoff Hurst, Martin Peters, Jack Burkett, Eddie Bovington and Alan Sealey. The signing of Johnny "Budgie" Byrne marked a milestone. At £65,000 it broke the transfer record and sent a signal to other clubs that West Ham intended to play with the big boys. Mid-table finishes of 8th, 12th and 14th may not have set the football world alight, but a golden era was about to dawn.

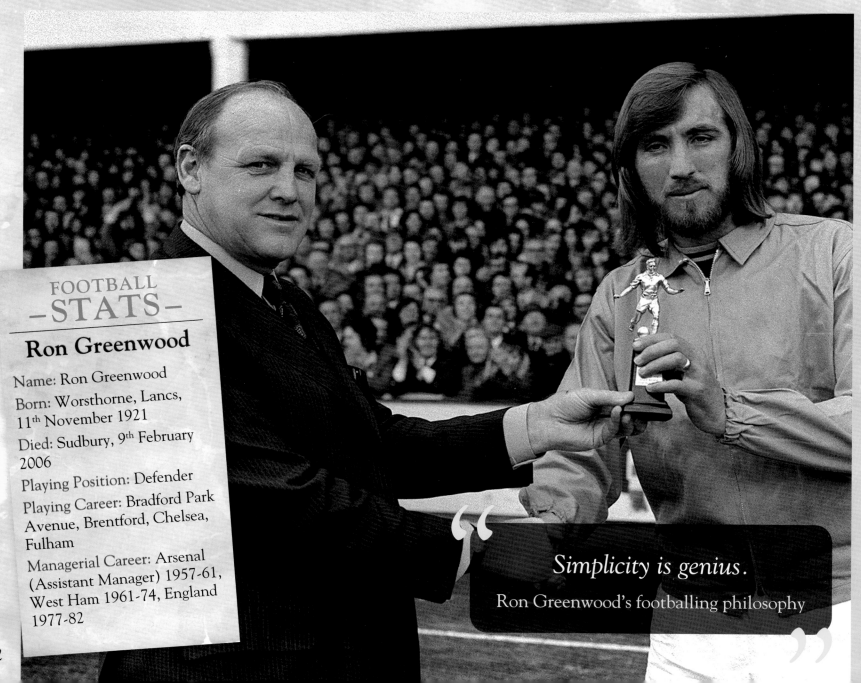

FOOTBALL -STATS-

Ron Greenwood

Name: Ron Greenwood

Born: Worsthorne, Lancs, 11th November 1921

Died: Sudbury, 9th February 2006

Playing Position: Defender

Playing Career: Bradford Park Avenue, Brentford, Chelsea, Fulham

Managerial Career: Arsenal (Assistant Manager) 1957-61, West Ham 1961-74, England 1977-82

Simplicity is genius.

Ron Greenwood's footballing philosophy

ABOVE: West Ham team photo, 1961.

BELOW: Ron Greenwood with two new signings in the 1961 pre season training, goalkeeper Lawrie Leslie and winger Ian Crawford.

1962

"*The crowds at West Ham have never been rewarded by results but they keep turning up because of the good football they see.*"

Ron Greenwood

LEFT: Upton Park closed, Boxing Day 1962.

RIGHT: Tony Scott and John Smith compete for the ball. Both players scored in the 4-4 draw at White Hart Lane, 22nd December 1962.

Singing in the Rain

LEFT: Bobby Moore and Johnny Byrne leaving West Ham's training ground, 1964.

Some of the West Ham team messing around before the Burnley game, 27th January 1964.

Ken Brown, Bobby Moore and Geoff Hurst find out who they will play in the semi-final of the FA Cup. Manchester United or Sunderland?

Hammers' hearts must have sunk when Manchester United came out of the hat. Although West Ham had beaten United 1-0 at Old Trafford earlier in the season, they had lost the return match at Upton Park 2-0 only a week before the semi-final was due to take place to a Manchester United team that was packed with reserve team players. Seven days later, the teams met at Hillsborough, on a quagmire of a pitch, with the Hammers fielding an unchanged side of Standen, Bond, Burkett, Bovington, Brown, Moore, Brabrook, Boyce, Byrne, Hurst and Sissons. A crowd of 65,000 saw a goalless first half, but the Hammers raced into a 2-0 lead early in the second half with a brace of goals scored by Ronnie Boyce, the first a 25-yard pile-driver. Bobby Moore, playing one of the best games of his career, almost single-handedly kept the Manchester United forwards at bay until Denis Law pulled one back for Manchester United in the 78th minute, but two minutes later Geoff Hurst clinched the game to make it 3-1. And with that, Wembley beckoned for the first time since 1923.

John Bond hugs goalkeeper Jim Standen after West Ham had beaten Manchester United in the FA Cup at Hillsborough to reach Wembley.

FA Cup 1964: The Road to Wembley

Third round	4th January	H	Charlton	3-0	Hurst 10, Brabrook 25, Sissons 89
Fourth round	25th January	A	Leyton Orient	1-1	Brabrook 43
Fourth round replay	29th January	H	Leyton Orient	3-0	Hurst 6, 8, Byrne 15
Fifth round	15th February	A	Swindon Town	3-1	Hurst 11, 77, Byrne 73
Quarter-final	29th February	H	Burnley	3-2	Sissons 57, Byrne 60, 68
Semi-final	14th March	Hillsborough	Manchester United	3-1	Boyce 56, 63, Hurst 80
Final	2nd May	Wembley	Preston North End	3-2	Sissons 12, Hurst 52, Boyce 90

West Ham team photo at Upton, April 1964, left to
right: Bobby Moore, Peter Brabook, Eddie Bovington, Jim
Standen, Geoff Hurst, John Bond, Johnny Byrne, John
Sissons, Jackie Burkett, Ronnie Boyce, Ken Brown.

West Ham captain Bobby Moore shakes hands with Preston North End captain Nobby Lawton before the match.

West Ham 3 Preston North End 2

West Ham entered Wembley Stadium as favourites to beat Preston North End, who had had a good season in the Second Division, finishing third and narrowly missing out on promotion. The Hammers' confidence was high as they had just celebrated Bobby Moore winning the accolade of Football Writers' Footballer of the Year. A capacity crowd enjoyed a thrilling final, reckoned to be the best since the famous Matthews final of 1953. Confident the Hammers may have been, but this didn't stop them falling behind twice to a vigorous Preston team who had no intention of becoming the West Ham whipping boys. Preston scored first through Holden after only 10 minutes but John Sissons immediately struck back only two minutes later. Five minutes before half-time Dawson put Preston ahead again, only for Geoff Hurst to head the ball home seven minutes after the restart. As the final whistle drew near, a replay beckoned until in the final minute of the game Peter Brabrook crossed and Ronnie Boyce headed home to give West Ham a 3-2 win and keep up the record of scoring three goals in every round.

MATCH FACTS
Date: 2nd May 1964
Venue: Wembley Stadium
Attendance: 100,000
Referee: A Holland
Line-up: Standen, Bond, Burkett, Bovington,
Brown, Moore, Brabrook, Boyce, Byrne,
Hurst, Sissons
Scorers: Sissons 12, Hurst 52, Boyce 90

ABOVE: Preston attack the West Ham goal.

LEFT: Geoff Hurst attacking the goal in the 1964 FA Cup final.

BELOW: Preston goalkeeper Alan Kelly looking at the ball over the line.

Boyce Seals It

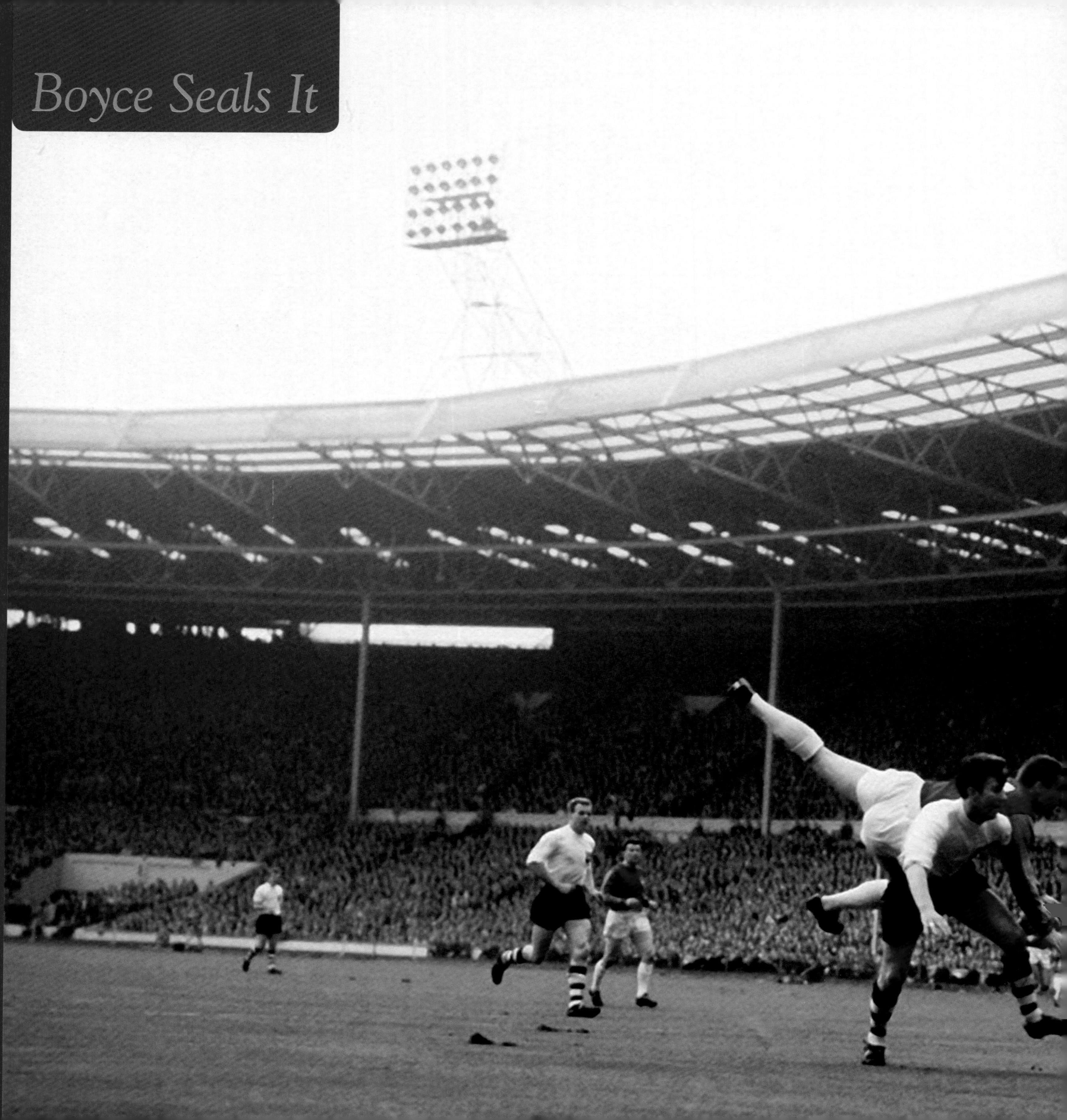

Bobby Moore holds up the FA Cup during the parade around East London.

Bobby Moore gives passing fans a touch of the FA Cup.

WAGs 1964 Style

ABOVE: The wives and girlfriends of the West Ham 1964 FA Cup final winning team.

–LEGENDS–

Ronnie Boyce

Ronnie Boyce was a local boy made good. He made his debut against Manchester United in October 1960 but it was during the period 1964–6 when he was at the peak of his powers. Hammers fans of the period will remember his two goals against Manchester United in the 1964 Cup semi-final which propelled West Ham to Wembley, and his winning goal against Preston in the final. But it was the following year against Sparta Prague in the European Cup Winners' Cup when he excelled himself, by taking over the captain's armband from an injured Bobby Moore and driving his team to an unlikely 3-2 aggregate victory and contributing two goals himself. His nickname was "Ticker" since he was the real heartbeat of the team, the Trevor Brooking of his day. He was a one club man and after his retirement in 1972 he stayed at the club in coaching and scouting roles. In February 1990 he took charge of first-team affairs for one match after the sacking of Lou Macari. A true Hammers great.

FOOTBALL –STATS–

Ronnie Boyce

Name: Ronald Boyce

Born: East Ham, 6th January 1943

Position: Midfielder

West Ham Playing Career: 1959-72

Club Appearances: 342

Goals: 29

England Appearances: 0

Goals: 0

> "He's a player's player – a tremendous worker, but people do not appreciate his value.
>
> Geoff Hurst on Ronnie Boyce"

Going Underground

The quiet man holding a parcel on the Tube train went unnoticed. He was Ron Greenwood, manager of West Ham, the parcel contained "The Cup". Ron, the team and the Cup had been to a film screening of the game, after which Ron returned to West Ham by Tube in April 1964.

Chasing the European Dream

John Bond throws his arms in triumph as his 25-yard shot thunders into the net for West Ham's first goal.

West Ham 2 Sparta Prague 0, 25th November 1964.

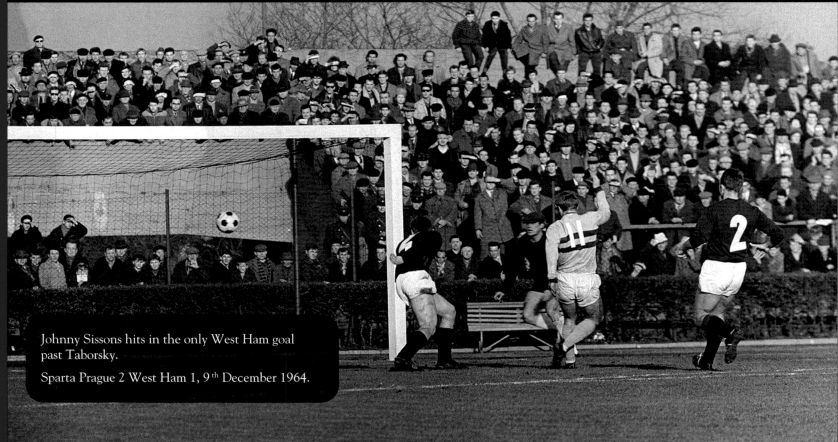

Johnny Sissons hits in the only West Ham goal past Taborsky.

Sparta Prague 2 West Ham 1, 9th December 1964.

West Ham's first, tentative footsteps into the exciting world of European football did not bode well. In the first round of the European Cup Winners' Cup West Ham drew the Belgian part-timers La Gantoise. It proved to be a difficult tie, with the Ghent-based team packing their defence in the home leg. Ronnie Boyce scored in a 1-0 away win, but at Upton Park the Hammers managed a feeble 1-1 draw to squeak through to the second round where they would meet Sparta Prague. They were another defensive-minded side and came to Upton Park to defend en masse. Midway into the second half John Bond belted a 30-yard volley into the Sparta net and Alan Sealey hit a second. In the away leg, a viciously dirty Sparta team managed a 2-1 win (Sissons scored for West Ham) but it was not enough to prevent West Ham's progress to the quarter-finals in March.

Bobby Moore returned from injury to face Swiss cup winners Lausanne, but it was Brian Dear who starred in both legs, scoring home and away. A 2-1 win and a thrilling 4-3 home win saw the Hammers through to a semi-final encounter with the highly rated Spanish cup winners and UEFA Cup holders Real Zaragoza. In the home leg the Hammers scored a narrow 2-1 win with the seemingly prolific Brian Dear scoring the first and "Budgie" Byrne adding the second. This was Dear's 10th goal in his first 10 games in a Hammers shirt. The away leg did not start well, with Real scoring and levelling the tie halfway through the first half, but it was Bobby Moore who rose to the occasion and led a changed formation with Hurst and Boyce shifting to a defensive role to stop the surging Real full-backs. It worked, and shortly after half-time Johnny Sissons scored the equalizer on the night, which turned out to be the tie-winning goal. Another trip to Wembley beckoned.

Jackie Burkett tackles Sparta defender Kraus.

West Ham also reached the semi-finals in 1966 but went out 5-2 on aggregate to West German Cup Winners, Borussia Dortmund.

West Ham 1 Borussia Dortmund 2, 5th April 1966.

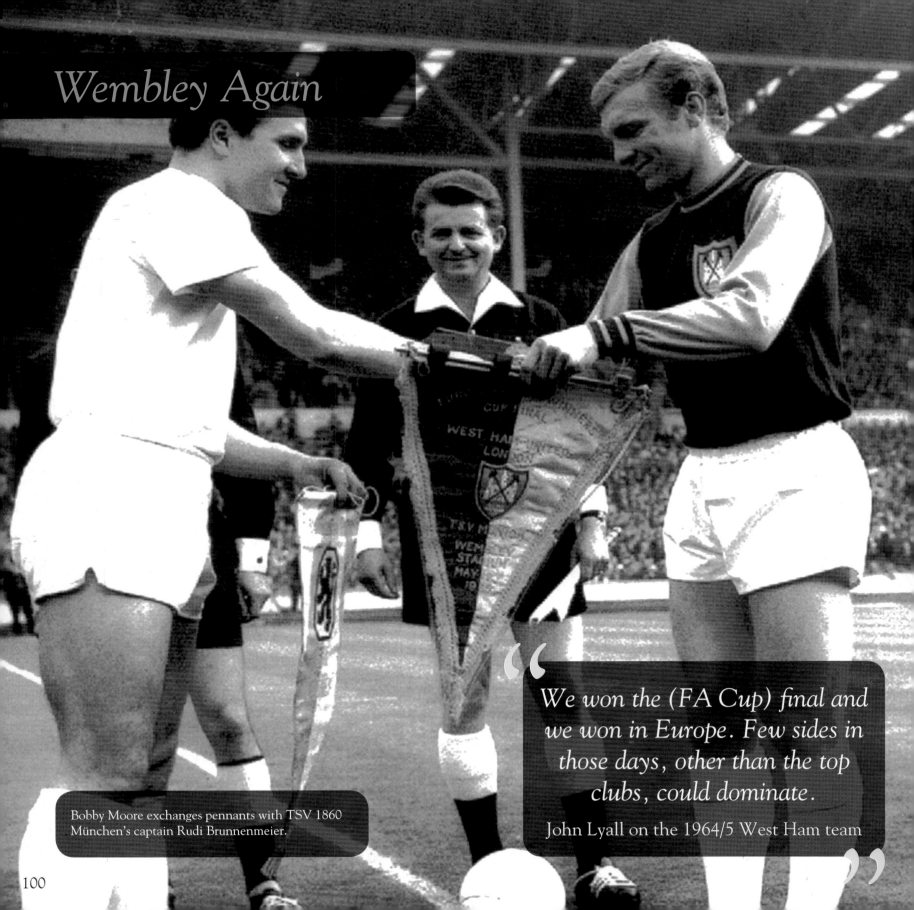

Wembley Again

Bobby Moore exchanges pennants with TSV 1860 München's captain Rudi Brunnenmeier.

We won the (FA Cup) final and we won in Europe. Few sides in those days, other than the top clubs, could dominate.

John Lyall on the 1964/5 West Ham team

Ron Greenwood said after the game "This was West Ham's greatest win", and who could contradict him? Even today, this match stands out as West Ham's ultimate achievement. On the face of it, West Ham were red hot favourites to win the game. Pseudo-home advantage at Wembley obviously counted in their favour, and their opponents were not highly regarded, despite the fact that they would go on to win the Bundesliga the next season. The first half was frustrating for the Hammers, mainly due to the superb performance of the 1860 keeper Peter Radenkovic, bizarrely wearing an all-black strip. He repelled everything West Ham threw at him, and many fans became nervous that a famous West Ham win was not meant to be.

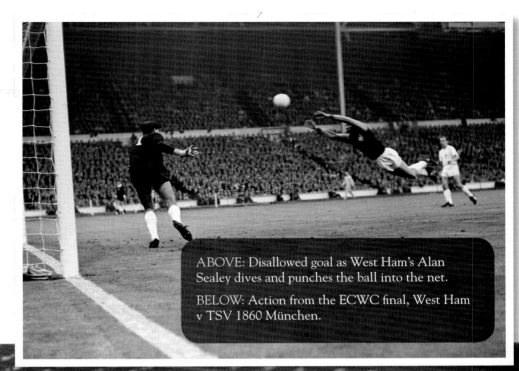

ABOVE: Disallowed goal as West Ham's Alan Sealey dives and punches the ball into the net.

BELOW: Action from the ECWC final, West Ham v TSV 1860 München.

EUROPEAN CUP WINNERS' CUP
FINAL TIE
TSV MÜNCHEN 1860
v
WEST HAM UNITED

MAY 19th 1965 WEMBLEY Kick-off 7.30 p.m.

MATCH FACTS
Date: 19th May 1965
Venue: Wembley Stadium
Attendance: 100,000
Referee: I Zsolt (Hungary)
Line-up: Standen, Kirkup, Burkett, Peters, Brown, Moore, Sealey, Boyce, Hurst, Dear, Sissons
Scorer: Sealey 69, 71

" *It was the way we won. For me, it was fulfilment.*

Ron Greenwood after the ECWC final "

Teamwork

But they hadn't reckoned with Alan Sealey, who had only ever been an intermittent first-team player since he joined the Hammers from Orient in 1960. In the 69th minute he scored the opening goal and two minutes later struck again to ensure a famous West Ham victory. The margin of victory could have been far wider, with Brian Dear having a goal disallowed and three open goals going begging. The teamwork displayed by the 11 West Ham players was remarked upon by all who saw the game, with Bobby Moore putting in an outstanding performance. Indeed, this West Ham team was named Team of the Year in the BBC Annual Sports Awards later in the year. Someone at the time said: "It doesn't get better than this." And it didn't.

ABOVE: Action from the match.

ABOVE RIGHT: West Ham goalkeeper Jim Standen makes a brilliant save from München inside-left Grosser.

RIGHT: Munich on the attack.

Sealey at the Double

ABOVE AND RIGHT: Alan Sealey cracks home his second goal in two minutes to kill München's hopes as Martin Peters looks on.

–LEGENDS–

Martin Peters MBE

Martin Peters was a product of the famous West Ham Academy. He made his full debut against Cardiff City on Good Friday in 1962. It was only in 1965 that he firmly established himself as a first-team regular and he played a leading part in the club's European Cup Winners' Cup campaign. He also scored in the 1966 doomed two-legged League Cup final against West Bromwich Albion. But it was the 1966 World Cup final in which he made his name, scoring England's second goal. He won 33 of his 67 England caps while playing for West Ham.

For a midfielder he had an astonishing scoring record, scoring 100 goals in 364 games from midfield. In 1968 he scored his one and only West Ham hat-trick against West Bromwich Albion and that season scored an astonishing 24 goals in 48 games, a record most strikers would have been proud of. Less than a year later he joined Spurs in a £200,000 deal that saw Jimmy Greaves come the other way. He went on to play 189 league games for Spurs, before finishing his career at Norwich City.

Scorecard:

1961-62	5-0
1962-63	39-9
1963-64	36-3
1964-65	47-6
1965-66	60-17
1966-67	49-16
1967-68	46-18
1968-69	48-24
1969-70	34-7

FOOTBALL –STATS–

Martin Peters

Name: Martin Stanford Peters

Born: Plaistow, 8th November 1943

Position: Midfielder

West Ham Playing Career: 1962-70

Club Appearances: 364

Goals: 100

England Appearances: 67

Goals: 20

> *Ten years ahead of his time.*
>
> Sir Alf Ramsey on Martin Peters

–LEGENDS– Sir Geoff Hurst MBE

The son of a lower league footballer, Geoff Hurst began his West Ham career as a wing-half. He played in that position for his first three years at Upton Park. But Ron Greenwood spotted his potential as a centre-forward – and the rest was history. In the 1962/3 season he scored 15 goals in 29 games, and 26 in 50 games the following season. In the World Cup year, excluding international goals he managed 40 goals in 59 games, a record that brought him firmly to the attention of England manager Alf Ramsey.

Hurst's club highlights must have been the goal he scored in the 1964 FA Cup final and the double hat-trick he scored against Sunderland in 1968, emulating a feat last achieved by Vic Watson 38 years earlier. In 1972 he left West Ham for Stoke City, where he played 108 games, scoring 30 goals. He finished his playing career at West Bromwich Albion in 1976 and three years later went on to manage Chelsea.

But it is his hat-trick in the 1966 World Cup final that keeps the name of Geoff Hurst forever tied to the most glorious day in the history of English football.

Scorecard:

Season	Score
1958-59	1-0
1959-60	4-0
1960-61	6-0
1961-62	27-1
1962-63	29-15
1963-64	50-26
1964-65	54-20
1965-66	59-40
1966-67	49-41
1967-68	44-25
1968-69	48-31
1969-70	42-18
1970-71	41-16
1971-72	48-16

BELOW LEFT: Geoff Hurst heads the third of one of his six goals past the Sunderland goalkeeper Jim Montogomery. West Ham 8 Sunderland 0, October 1968.

FOOTBALL –STATS–

Geoff Hurst

Name: Sir Geoffrey Charles Hurst MBE

Born: Ashton under Lyme, 8th December 1941

Position: Centre-forward

West Ham Playing Career: 1960-72

Club Appearances: 501

Goals: 249

England Appearances: 49

Goals: 24

" *I am looking for someone big and strong and not afraid to work.* "

Ron Greenwood on why he converted Geoff Hurst from a half-back to a centre-forward in 1962.

West Ham 4 West Germany 2

Saturday 30th July 1966 was the finest day in the history of English football. It was the day West Ham won the World Cup at Wembley. Bobby Moore was captain, Martin Peters scored once, Geoff Hurst scored a hat-trick in a 4-2 victory. OK, there were eight other players from other clubs there too, but no one can seriously doubt West Ham's amazing contribution to England's World Cup triumph.

Geoff Hurst scores that infamous disputed goal.

117

After the Lord Mayor's Show

Having won the FA Cup, European Cup Winners' Cup and the World Cup (OK, slight exaggeration, but you know what I mean) great things were expected of West Ham in the second half of the 1960s, but just like our dreams those expectations faded and died. The Board failed to invest in newer and better players, missing out on Alex Stepney, Terry Venables and Peter Bonetti among others. The club also had the chance to sign England goalkeeper Gordon Banks, but instead Ron Greenwood plumped for Kilmarnock stopper Bobby Ferguson. In May 1967 Billy Bonds was signed from Charlton, arguably Greenwood's most significant purchase in his 13 years as manager.

The 1965-66 team.

In an away match at Liverpool on 15th November 1969 Billy Bonds receives treatment for a leg injury. Ron Greenwood runs on to the pitch to inspect it himself.

Bobby Moore shakes hands with Bobby Charlton before kick off. West Ham 1 Manchester United 3, 2nd September 1967.

BELOW: On his debut, West Ham's newly signed goalkeeper Bobby Ferguson steals the ball from Wednesday's Jim McCalliog, watched by a concerned Bobby Moore. West Ham went on to lose the game 3-2.

I remember Wembley, When West Ham beat West Germany, Martin one and Geoffrey Three, And Bobby got the OBE.

Terrace chant in 1966/7

119

West Ham team photo, July 1968.

West Ham seemed to score at will, but defensively remained somewhat of a shambles. The end of the 1967/8 season said goodbye to the famous Chicken Run as it was replaced, at a cost of £200,000, by the East Stand with 3,500 seats and covered terracing. Perhaps the most notable match of the era was an 8-0 thrashing of Sunderland in which Geoff Hurst scored a double hat-trick.

Geoff Hurst heads one of his six goals past the Sunderland goalkeeper Jim Montgomery. West Ham 8 Sunderland 0 , 19th October 1968.

The new "Old Chicken Run", 1972.

–LEGENDS–

Johnny Byrne

Johnny Byrne was undoubtedly one of the greatest players ever to pull on a Hammers shirt. The fact that he has been eclipsed by the World Cup trio of Hurst, Moore and Peters should not hide the fact that for five years in the 1960s he was at the centre of every success the club enjoyed. Having scored eight England goals in 11 appearances (including a hat-trick in a 4-3 win against Eusebio's Portugal) he was desperately unlucky not to make the final World Cup squad and he never really recovered from the disappointment. He was signed from Crystal Palace in March 1962, having scored 95 goals in 220 games for the lower league side. The £65,000 transfer fee was a British record. He was a member of the 1964 Cup winning team and was voted Hammer of the Year that season. However, a knee injury forced him out of the 1965 European Cup Winners' Cup final, although a year later he was to score a goal in the second leg of the League Cup final against West Bromwich Albion. In February 1967 he rejoined Crystal Palace and was later to play for Fulham before moving to South Africa.

Scorecard:

1961-62	11-1
1962-63	37-14
1963-64	45-33
1964-65	45-30
1965-66	37-17
1966-67	32-13

The English Di Stefano.

Ron Greenwood on Budgie Byrne

FOOTBALL –STATS–

Budgie Byrne

Name: John Joseph Byrne

Born: West Horsley, 13th May 1939

Died: South Africa, 27th October 1999

Position: Striker

West Ham Playing Career: 1962-67

Club Appearances: 207

Goals: 108

England Appearances: 11

Goals: 8

–LEGENDS–

Bryan "Pop" Robson

In any West Ham team of the 1970s surely Bryan "Pop" Robson would be one of the first names on the team sheet. Signed by Ron Greenwood in February 1971 for £120,000 from Newcastle, he proved a highly popular addition to the strike force. He was top scorer in two of his initial three seasons at Upton Park, but after an injury hit season in which he scored only eight goals he headed back to the northeast in an £80,000 move to Sunderland in July 1974. Two years later John Lyall was struggling with an injury crisis and he re-signed Robson for £80,000. It was an inspired move. In 1979 Robson was back at Roker Park for the second of his three stints there. It meant that having missed out on West Ham's 1975 FA Cup final win, he would also miss out in 1980. But to anyone who knows anything about the history of West Ham in the 1970s, he remains a legend.

Scorecard:

1970-71	14-3
1971-72	56-14
1972-73	46-28
1973-74	24-8
1976-77	32-14
1977-78	41-11
1978-79	42-26

FOOTBALL –STATS–

Pop Robson

Name: Bryan Stanley Robson

Born: Sunderland, 11th November 1945

Position: Centre-forward

West Ham Playing Career: 1971-74, 1976-79

Club Appearances: 255

Goals: 104

England Appearances: 0

Goals: 0

"When you are a scorer, the public judge you on how many goals you get rather than how well you are playing and that's just another pressure you have to learn to live and cope with."

Pop Robson

Difficult Times

West Ham entered the 1970s with fans feeling uncertain about the club's future and the Board's ambition. The 1970/1 season saw the Hammers finishing one place above the relegation zone. The fining of Bobby Moore, Clyde Best and Jimmy Greaves for partying in a Blackpool nightclub the night before a game seemed to indicate that all was not well behind the scenes. Bobby Moore and Ron Greenwood were said to have a cool relationship. Having signed Bryan Robson from Newcastle Ron Greenwood instituted a purge at the end of the season, giving free transfers to seven players and transfer listing four others. Tommy Taylor and John McDowell emerged as top-class defenders.

RIGHT: Bryan "Pop" Robson tries to take a shot but is blocked by Roy McFarland. West Ham 3 Derby County 3, 22nd January 1972.

BELOW RIGHT: Jimmy Greaves scores for West Ham in a 2-2 draw with Ipswich, 20th March 1970.

BELOW: Billy Bonds challenges George Best of Man United at Upton Park, 3rd April 1971. The Hammers won 2-1 with goals from Hurst and Robson.

Jimmy Greaves gets a helping hand from a muddy Geoff Hurst.

125

The Early 1970s

One of the most memorable matches of the early 1970s was the multi-replay League Cup semi-final in January 1972 against Stoke City. In the second replay at Old Trafford Bobby Moore had to take over in goal from the concussed Bobby Ferguson. He saved a penalty but couldn't grab the follow-up, and in the end Stoke triumphed 3-2 in a pulsating match.

League Cup semi-final 1971/2 v Stoke City

8th December	Upton Park	2-1
	Hurst 28, Best 62	
15th December	Victoria Ground	0-1
5th January	Hillsborough	0-0
26th January	Old Trafford	2-3
	Bonds 39, Brooking 46	

LEFT: Leeds goalkeeper Gary Sprake catches the high ball under pressure from Billy Bonds. Bonds scored in the 2-2 draw, 31st March 1972.

RIGHT: Bobby Moore beats Chelsea's Chris Garland in a tussle for the ball. West Ham 3 Chelsea 1, September 1972.

BELOW: West Ham team photo, January 1972. McDowell, Heffer, Ferguson, Grotier, Brooking, Lampard, Bonds, Llewellyn, Taylor, Stephenson, Moore, Eustace, Ayris, Redknapp, Boyce, Hurst, Robson, Howe.

Black Gold

John Charles was the first black player to play for West Ham. He made his debut on 4th May 1963. Ten years later his brother Clive played alongside Clyde Best and Ade Coker in a 2-0 victory against Spurs on 1st April 1973. It was the first time three black players had appeared in a West Ham team. Nowadays, no one would blink an eye at the prospect, but at the time it was fairly revolutionary. Clyde Best was a pioneer and role model. He played 186 league games for West Ham between 1968 and 1976, scoring 47 goals.

> *The soccer ball doesn't care what colour you are.*
>
> Clyde Best

Clyde Best with Johnny Ayris in a November 1971 home league game against Sheffield United.

Ringing the Changes

The 1972/3 season saw a revival in the Hammers' fortunes and they finished sixth, this despite the departure of Geoff Hurst to Stoke City and Harry Redknapp to Bournemouth. Much of the success was due to the goalscoring exploits of Pop Robson who scored 17 goals in 25 games, finishing with 28. But the success was not to last. The following season saw the knives sharpening for Ron Greenwood, particularly after he had the temerity to drop Bobby Moore. In March the unthinkable happened and Bobby Moore left Upton Park for Fulham for a fee of £50,000. An 18th-place finish and the subsequent loss of Pop Robson to Sunderland did not seem to auger well for the future.

ABOVE: West Ham in training, 6th April 1972: Moore, Bonds, Stephenson, Hurst, Robson and Best.

LEFT: Clyde Best being challenged for the ball by Dennis Clarke. West Ham 3 Huddersfield 0, 4th March 1972.

RIGHT: Harry Redknapp in action during the FA Cup fourth-round replay match against Hereford United at Upton Park, which the Hammers won 3-1 due to a Hurst hat-trick, 14th February 1972.

131

—LEGENDS—

Bobby Moore OBE

There's not a single West Ham fan who would deny Bobby Moore the status of the greatest player ever to have played at Upton Park. He remains a hero to this day. Bobby Moore joined West Ham as a youth player in 1956, making his debut against Manchester United two years later in West Ham's first season back in the First Division. It was in the 1960/1 season that he established himself as a first-choice central defender. At the end of the next season he was called up for the England World Cup squad in Chile, making his debut in a 4-0 pre tournament drubbing of Peru and went on to play in every game. A year later he became England's youngest ever captain, a position he held for a decade. In three successive Wembley appearances from 1964 he lifted the FA Cup, the European Cup Winners' Cup and the World Cup. Four years later he captained England's World Cup bid in Mexico and in February 1973 he won his 100th cap and broke West Ham's all-time appearance record. But only a year later, he was to leave West Ham in a £50,000 transfer to Fulham. It truly was the end of an era.

"My captain, my leader, my right-hand man. He was the spirit and the heartbeat of the team. A cool, calculating footballer I could trust with my life. He was the supreme professional, the best I ever worked with. Without him England would never have won the World Cup.

Sir Alf Ramsey

"Keep forever asking yourself: 'If I get the ball now, who will I give it to?'

Malcolm Allison's advice to Bobby Moore.

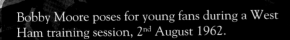

Bobby Moore poses for young fans during a West Ham training session, 2nd August 1962.

FOOTBALL –STATS–

Bobby Moore

Name: Robert Frederick Chelsea Moore OBE

Born: Barking, 8th April 1941

Died: London, 24th February 1993

Position: Central defender

West Ham Playing Career: 1958-74

Club Appearances: 646

Goals: 27

England Appearances: 108

Goals: 2

The John Lyall Era
1974-1989

John Lyall encourages striker Bobby Gould during a 2-1 victory over Burnley in March 1975.

For John Lyall, reaching the FA Cup final in his first season was a massive achievement, which was all the more poignant when he realized that West Ham would be up against Fulham and Bobby Moore. Again. It was by no means a classic final. Fulham had the better of the first half, but two spills by Fulham goalkeeper Peter Mellor presented Alan Taylor with an opportunity to score another two goals from close range, which he accepted without further ado. Bobby Moore put in a fine performance and had it not been for Taylor, he would have probably been man of the match. But Moore knew that the record books rarely remember the defeated and it was a sorry sight to see him trudge off the field alone with his thoughts. Meanwhile, though, the East End prepared to party!

RIGHT: Trevor Brooking and Bobby Moore in action during the 1975 FA Cup final.

Beating Bobby Moore

Billy Bonds battles for the ball with Bobby Moore.

Bobby Moore embraced by players from his old club after the match.

Let the Party Begin

Billy Bonds lifts the cup after the presentation.

ABOVE: Alan Taylor, Trevor Brooking and Billy Bonds show off the trophy to the crowd below at Newham Town Hall.

BELOW: West Ham fans try to get a good view above the crowds during the victory parade through East London.

Another European Tour

Having won the European Cup Winners' Cup in 1965, a decade later West Ham again reached the final. Victory wasn't to be, but the journey to the final against Anderlecht in the Heysel Stadium at the beginning of May 1976 was certainly an entertaining one. The competition began with a 5-2 aggregate win over Lahden Reipas from Finland.

RIGHT THREE: West Ham 3 Lahden Reipas 0, 1st October 1975.

Next up was a trip to Armenia to meet Ararat Yerevan. The Soviet side scored first after the ball was headed out of a startled Mervyn Day's hands. Alan Taylor equalized, but the Hammers had to wait for the return tie to secure progress to the next round with a 3-1 win.

RIGHT THREE: West Ham 3 Ararat Yerevan 1, 5th November 1975.

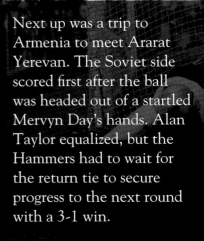

—LEGENDS— Phil Parkes

West Ham paid a world record fee for a goalkeeper of £565,000 when they signed Phil Parkes from QPR in 1979 and it was money well spent. For seven years he made the position his own. He played a key part in the promotion-winning season of 1980/1, keeping 22 clean sheets, a performance which won him the coveted Hammer of the Year award. At the age of 36, he enjoyed perhaps his finest season among the Boys of '86 and helped the team secure the club's highest ever league finish of third. Age, and dodgy knees, were catching up with him, but in the last two years of the decade he came to the rescue when his replacement Allen McKnight proved a less than safe pair of hands. He left the Hammers on a free transfer to John Lyall's new club, Ipswich Town. In 2003 a poll of West Ham fans voted Parkes West Ham's greatest ever goalkeeper.

FOOTBALL —STATS—

Phil Parkes

Name: Philip Benjamin Neil Frederick Parkes

Born: Sedgley, Staffs, 8th August 1950

Position: Goalkeeper

West Ham Playing Career: 1979-90

Club Appearances: 436

Goals: 0

England Appearances: 1

Goals: 0

The **1978** Team

LEFT: West Ham team photo, September 1978.

Kevin Lock, Billy Bonds, Bill Green, Mervyn Day,
Tommy Taylor, Trevor Brooking, Keith Robson,
Alan Curbishley, Billy Jennings, Alan Taylor,
Bobby Ferguson, Frank Lampard, John McDowell,
Mick McGiven, Yilmaz Orhan, John Ayris, Pat
Holland, Graham Paddon, Keith Coleman.

Heading Down

As the start of the 1976/7 season drew closer, Hammers fans were optimistic that the achievements of the previous two seasons could be built on. But it was not to be. The club was in a state of transition with several changes in the backroom staff, chief among them the departure of the long-serving Wally St Pier, who had been at the club for 47 years as a player scout and youth policy director. Injury problems led to a desperate start with only two wins by early November. The second was a memorable 5-3 trouncing of Spurs. Pop Robson was re-signed from Sunderland and went on to score 14 goals in 30 games, although the acquisition of former Arsenal star striker John Radford proved less successful. Wins against Manchester United and Liverpool followed by the end of the year, but that was it. West Ham never climbed above 17th throughout the season and spent most of it mired in the bottom four. It was only towards the end of the season that a chink of light broke through. Three wins, nine draws and only one defeat in the final 13 games gave some hope, and an emphatic 4-2 victory over Manchester United on the final day of the season guaranteed safety for another year. But there was one bright moment – the emergence of a star midfielder. His name? Alan Devonshire.

LEFT AND ABOVE: West Ham 4 Manchester United 2, 16th May 1977.

BELOW: Geoff Pike scores to put West Ham 2-1 ahead.

Carl Harris fends off Tommy Taylor as he sets up another Leeds attack, with Paul Brush looking on from behind.

1977/8 proved no more successful than the previous season had been for West Ham and culminated in the relegation of the East London team. Uncertainty over the futures of several key players, including the talismanic Trevor Brooking, and the departure of Ron Greenwood to manage England all helped to create nervousness among the playing staff. West Ham lost their first three league games. Few funds were available for new players due to the amount of money which had to be spent on the ground to comply with new safety laws. The prolific Derek Hales had been signed from Charlton at the start of the season but he never recaptured the form he had shown for the Addicks. Things improved when David Cross arrived from West Bromwich Albion, but it was in defence that West Ham had problems, shipping goals with gay abandon. The unthinkable happened and Mervyn Day was dropped, with Bobby Ferguson being recalled. Again, the Hammers went on a winning run, winning five out of six games in March, but they flattered to deceive. Although they finished the season above the bottom three, Wolves still had games to play and managed to pull above the Hammers, who now faced Second Division football for the first time in 20 years.

" *I just want you to know that I want to stay at West Ham and help get the team back to the First Division.*

Trevor Brooking, speaking to John Lyall after West Ham were relegated in May 1978. "

Vince Hillaire of Palace clashes with Pop Robson during the match. Final score: West Ham United 1 Crystal Palace 1.

Another Cup Run Beckons...

The five years following the 1975 FA Cup win were less than lucrative silverware-wise for the Hammers. Maybe 1980 would be different. Languishing for a second season in Division Two, the club's priority was a speedy return to the top flight. This didn't happen; instead, the Hammers finished seventh. But the 1979/80 season will always be remembered by Hammers fans for other reasons – the main one being a rare Trevor Brooking header. But we're getting ahead of ourselves. West Ham's cup run started shakily, needing a replay at Upton Park to despatch West Bromwich Albion and with Trevor Brooking scoring the crucial goal. Next up were East London neighbours Orient, whom West Ham narrowly beat 3-2 in a thriller at Bloomfield Road courtesy of a double strike by newly signed defender Ray Stewart. In the fifth round the Hammers beat Swansea 2-0 with two late goals from 17-year-old Paul Allen and the prolific David Cross. Another home tie followed against Aston Villa, with Ray Stewart scoring a last-minute trademark penalty, one of 14 goals he scored in his first season at Upton Park.

–LEGENDS–

Frank Lampard

Frank Lampard was a true West Ham servant. Playing 551 league games between 1967 and 1985 he was one of the greatest full-backs ever to pull on the claret and blue shirt, but despite winning two England caps he never quite got the accolades he deserved. Perhaps his greatest moment in a Hammers shirt was when he scored the goal in the 1980 FA Cup semi-final which took West Ham to Wembley. His celebratory run around the Elland Road corner flag still brings a smile, and a tear, to every Hammers fan who remembers that triumphant day. It went some way to exorcising the memory of the crippling stomach injury he suffered in the 1976 European Cup Winners' final when his stubbed back pass gifted Anderlecht their opening goal. Only 11 years after leaving West Ham on a free transfer, another Frank Lampard took to the field, his son Frank Jr.

Playing in the 1975 Charity Shield.

With Billy Bonds and David Essex.

FOOTBALL –STATS–

Frank Lampard

Name: Frank Richard George Lampard

Born: East Ham, 20th September 1948

Position: Left-back

West Ham Playing Career: 1967-85

Club Appearances: 774

Goals: 22

England Appearances: 2

Goals: 0

Road to Wembley

In a repeat of their 1975 experience, the Hammers needed two games to get through the semi-finals, this time against Everton. In the first game at Villa Park, Stuart Pearson equalized in the 70th minute of a bad tempered game. The replay at Elland Road was scoreless after 90 minutes. Alan Devonshire put the Hammers ahead only for Everton's Bob Latchford to equalize seven minutes before time. It was the unlikely figure of Frank Lampard, deputizing for the injured Billy Bonds, who headed the winner. Next up, Arsenal. At Wembley.

Alan Devonshire tangles with Everton's Andy King and gives away a penalty. West Ham 1 Everton 1, in the FA Cup semi-final, 12th April 1980.

FA Cup 1980: The Road to Wembley

Round	Date	Venue	Opponent	Score	Scorers
Third round	5th January	A	West Brom	1-1	Pearson 33
Third round replay	8th January	H	West Brom	2-1	Pike 53, Brooking 83
Fourth round	26th January	A	Orient	3-2	Gray og 28, Stewart 34p, 81
Fifth round	16th February	H	Swansea	2-0	Allen 85, Cross 86
Quarter-final	8th March	H	Aston Villa	1-0	Stewart 89
Semi-final	12th April	Villa Park	Everton	1-1	Pearson 70
Semi-final replay	16th April	Elland Road	Everton	2-1aet	Devonshire 94, Lampard 118
Final	10th May	Wembley	Arsenal	1-0	Brooking 13

ABOVE: David Cross looks on as Stuart Pearson's shot goes over the line to earn a replay.

LEFT: Frank Lampard dives to head in West Ham's winning goal against Everton. He then runs round and round the corner flag in celebration in a scene Hammers fans remember to this day.

—LEGENDS—

Sir Trevor Brooking CBE

Trevor Brooking was one of the last of a dying breed – the one club footballer. It is hard to think that he made his first-team debut in 1967, scoring nine goals that season in 25 league appearances. But it wasn't until 1971/2 that he became an automatic first-team choice, and even then he was once transfer listed as Ron Greenwood wasn't sure he was the real deal. He was a key part of the 1975 Cup-winning team and five years later came the moment every West Ham fan will remember him for – his famous headed goal which won the 1980 FA Cup against Arsenal. His commitment to the club was personified when he made clear he would not leave, even when the Hammers were relegated in 1978. He won Hammer of the Year on four occasions in the 1970s including in three consecutive years (1976-78). He made his England debut in 1974 at Wembley against Argentina and bowed out eight years later in a brief appearance as a substitute in the 1982 World Cup finals. He remains one of the true gentlemen of football and can be seen at virtually every West Ham home game. He may now be a Knight of the Realm and a Commander of the British Empire, but he remains at heart a Hammer.

Have I got anything bad to say about him? Well, he got cautioned by the referee at Burnley once.

John Lyall on Trevor Brooking

With wife Hilkka and daughter Colette in 1980.

> " *West Ham was always regarded as a family club. I had two managers in 17 years.* "
>
> Trevor Brooking

Playing in the 1-1 home draw with Leicester City, 20th September 1973.

Scorecard:

Season	
1967-68	28-9
1968-69	37-8
1969-70	23-4
1970-71	20-2
1971-72	54-7
1972-73	44-11
1973-74	41-6
1974-75	50-5
1975-76	49-9
1976-77	47-4
1977-78	39-4
1978-79	22-2
1979-80	54-6
1980-81	52-10
1981-82	43-9
1982-83	1-0
1983-84	43-6

> " *He floats like a butterfly and stings like one.* "
>
> Brian Clough on Trevor Brooking in 1980

FOOTBALL –STATS–

Trevor Brooking

Name: Trevor David Brooking

Born: Barking, 2nd October 1948

Position: Midfielder

West Ham Playing Career: 1967-84

Club Appearances: 647

Goals: 102

England Appearances: 47

Goals: 5

West Ham 1
Arsenal 0

If ever there has been an underdog in an FA Cup final, West Ham were it. Arsenal were appearing in their third successive final, having won a 3-2 thriller against Manchester United a year earlier. John Lyall provided further evidence of his tactical nouse by deciding to play David Cross as a lone striker, with Stuart Pearson, signed from Manchester United at the start of the season withdrawing into a five-man midfield. In the 13th minute, Alan Devonshire crossed from the left-hand byline, the ball came to David Cross whose shot cannoned off an Arsenal defender into the path of Stuart Pearson. He let rip with a fierce shot which was then guided into the net off the head of Trevor Brooking who was celebrating his 500th Hammers appearance.

West Ham then defended their lead magnificently for 77 minutes. The lowlight of the game came in the 87th minute. Arsenal were leaving gaping holes in their defence as they pushed forward in vain attempts to score an equalizer. West Ham's Paul Allen, the youngest player ever to appear in a Cup final at that point, broke free into the Arsenal half and looked to be heading for a one-to-one with Arsenal keeper Pat Jennings. Unfortunately he never got that far, as he was cynically hacked down by Gunners defender Willie Young. Astonishingly, he escaped with a yellow, rather than a red card. It was a famous victory for West Ham, and 30 years on, they have yet to match it.

RIGHT: Trevor Brooking celebrates scoring West Ham's Cup final goal.

162

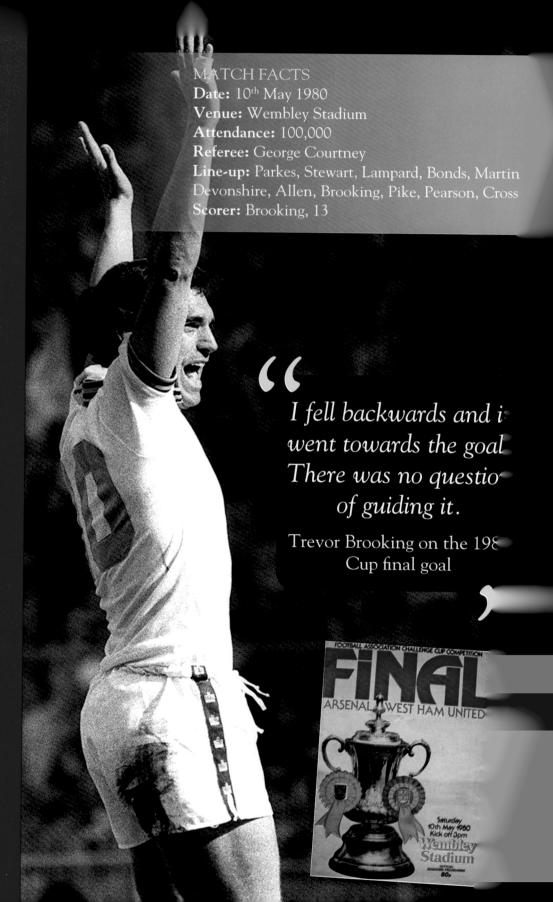

MATCH FACTS
Date: 10th May 1980
Venue: Wembley Stadium
Attendance: 100,000
Referee: George Courtney
Line-up: Parkes, Stewart, Lampard, Bonds, Martin Devonshire, Allen, Brooking, Pike, Pearson, Cross
Scorer: Brooking, 13

"
I fell backwards and i went towards the goal There was no questio of guiding it.

Trevor Brooking on the 198 Cup final goal

> "
> I will always be remembered as the player who cried at Wembley. When I was collecting my winner's medal there were tears in my eyes. Most West Ham fans I speak to still recall it vividly. And they always mention the moment I was brought down by Willie Young. It's the first thing they remember.
> "
>
> Paul Allen

Paul Allen downed by Willie Young during the 1980 FA Cup final.

Frank Lampard, Liam Brady and Alvin Martin.

ABOVE: Brooking in defence as Arsenal launch an attack during the West Ham v Arsenal Cup final, 1980.

West Ham pose for a team photo with the trophy to celebrate their win, May 1980. Pictured are Phil Parkes, Trevor Brooking, Billy Bonds, Alvin Martin, Pat Holland, Paul Brush, Jimmy Neighbour, David Cross, Stuart Pearson, Alan Devonshire, Paul Allen, Ray Stewart, Geoff Pike and Frank Lampard.

–LEGENDS–

David Cross

David Cross joined West Ham in December 1977 for a club record fee of £180,000. He had a no nonsense, physical and totally fearless style of play which soon led to him being christened by West Ham fans. Cross had many memorable outings for the Hammers but will be remembered primarily for two games. The 1980 Cup final was a memorable game for David Cross, not because he scored – he didn't – but a few minutes before kick-off, John Lyall took him aside and told him he would play as a lone striker in front of a five-man midfield. A shocked Cross tried to take in the news as he trooped out onto the famous Wembley turf. He played his heart out and was the unsung hero of the game. In September 1981 he achieved the feat of scoring all the goals in a memorable away win against Spurs. And it is for that which makes him a true Hammers legend.

"

As the 1979/80 season unfolded a running joke emerged between myself and our physio, Rob Jenkins. Whenever we travelled to an away game on the train or coach and saw a pig in a farm or field I would invariably score and we would usually win. This became so prevalent that one day Rob bought me a miniature plastic pig as a good luck charm. The following season the pig made its way to every game and I netted 34 goals and won the Golden Boot as we returned to the top flight.

As all West Ham fans know, 1980 was the year we played Arsenal in the FA Cup final and being such a big game I decided that I should do something more than just take the pig to the match. I therefore carried the pig in my hand throughout the full 90 minutes that day and thanks to John Lyall's tactical brilliance and Trevor Brooking's head we ended up winning the Cup.

I had never been particularly superstitious, in fact my only superstition was to not be superstitious! Those supporters that remember the side I played in will know that John Lyall had put together a wonderful group of footballers who played the West Ham way and because of that quality the chances to score would always be there. But on the 10th May 1980, in my left hand at Wembley, was the pig.

"

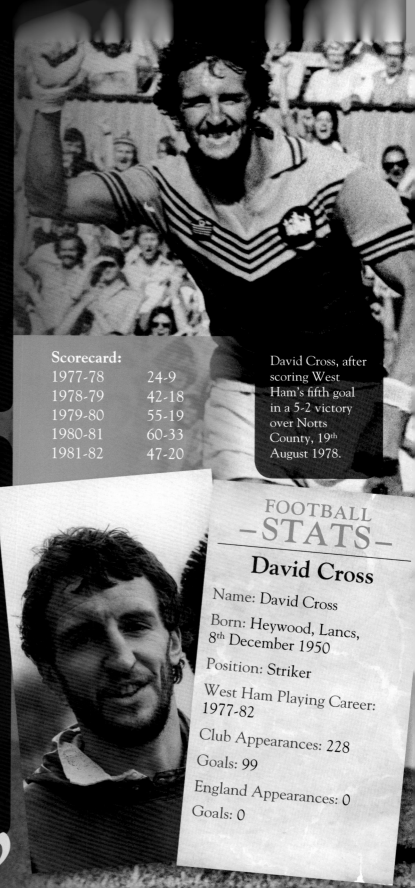

Scorecard:

Season	Stats
1977-78	24-9
1978-79	42-18
1979-80	55-19
1980-81	60-33
1981-82	47-20

David Cross, after scoring West Ham's fifth goal in a 5-2 victory over Notts County, 19th August 1978.

FOOTBALL –STATS–

David Cross

Name: David Cross

Born: Heywood, Lancs, 8th December 1950

Position: Striker

West Ham Playing Career: 1977-82

Club Appearances: 228

Goals: 99

England Appearances: 0

Goals: 0

–LEGENDS–

Alan Devonshire

Alan Devonshire's silky skills would have graced any team of the 1970s and 1980s. The fact that he plied his trade at Upton Park is something all Hammers fans have cause to be grateful for. He was signed from non-league Southall in September 1976 for a mere £5,000. Playing on the left-hand side of midfield he terrorized opposition defences. Never a prolific goalscorer (only 29 in 358 league appearances), he didn't need to be as he, together with Trevor Brooking, made it his job to lay on the goalscoring opportunities for his strikers. It was a travesty that he only won eight England caps, but injury blighted his career. He missed the entire 1984/5 season, but returned to play a starring role in 1985/6, the season West Ham finished third. But in the next four seasons he only managed 48 appearances before he moved to Watford to end his career. He was undoubtedly one of the finest midfielders ever to play at Upton Park.

BELOW: Always a target for the hatchet man, Alan Devonshire suffered from a huge number of injuries. He is pictured here before being stretchered off in an FA Cup fourth round tie with Wigan in January 1984. West Ham won 1-0.

FOOTBALL –STATS–

Alan Devonshire

Name: Alan Devonshire

Born: Park Royal, 13th April 1956

Position: Midfielder

West Ham Playing Career: 1976-90

Club Appearances: 448

Goals: 32

England Appearances: 8

Goals: 0

Promotion

Basking in the glory of FA Cup success, the season began at Wembley with a 1-0 loss to Liverpool in the Charity Shield. Everyone expected West Ham to win promotion to the top flight the following season, and they duly obliged. And they did it with style, winning the Second Division championship by a margin of 13 points from second placed Notts County. West Ham remained unbeaten in their last 18 matches, and with a record points total of 66 John Lyall was deservedly named Second Division manager of the year. David Cross and Paul Goddard, signed for £800,000 from QPR, piled in the goals and West Ham lost only four games all season.

RIGHT: Left to right: Paul Brush, Ray Stewart, David Cross and Frank Lampard celebrate with bottles of bubbly after winning the Second Division championship to hoist them back into the First Division.

SEASON FACTS:
P42 W28 D10 L4 F79 A29 Pts 66 – **Position** 1st
Regular side: P Parkes, R Stewart, B Bonds, F Lampard, A Martin, G Pike, P Holland, T Brooking, A Devonshire, P Goddard, D Cross
Top scorers: David Cross 27, Paul Goddard 21
Captain: Billy Bonds
Hammer of the Year: Phil Parkes

" When I scored it was like pulling the pin on a hand grenade, the way they came at us.

Paul Goddard

"

173

Moving on up?

As in 1965 and 1975, Hammers fans expected great things following the 1980 Cup final triumph. They wanted the Board to invest in new players and push the team on to bigger and better things in the league. Only François van der Elst and Neil Orr were signed at the beginning of West Ham's first season back in the top flight, but it was to be a good season for the Hammers. A 4-0 away thumping of Spurs was the highlight, where David Cross scored all four goals. Finishes of eighth, ninth and ninth proved that West Ham were heading in the right direction. There was a blip in 1984/5 but with the signing of Tony Gale, West Ham's side looked increasingly formidable. The 1985/6 season proved just how.

RIGHT: Pat Holland was one of West Ham's stars of the 1970s, scoring 32 goals in 296 games. A gritty and skilful right-winger, he played in the 1975 Cup final but cruelly missed out on the 1980 final due to injury.

BELOW: English league Division One match. Stoke City 5 West Ham United 2, November 1982.

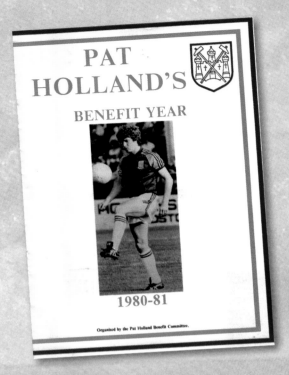

PAT HOLLAND'S

BENEFIT YEAR

1980-81

Organised by the Pat Holland Benefit Committee.

ABOVE: Tony Cottee scores West Ham's opening goal in the 26th minute of his league debut against Spurs. West Ham 3 Tottenham Hotspur 0, 1st January 1983.

ABOVE: Tony Cottee looks on as West Ham score in an FA Cup fourth round replay. West Ham 2 Crystal Palace 0, 31st January 1984.

BELOW: Ray "Tonka" Stewart celebrates yet another of his trademark penalties during a 3-0 win against Notts County in the fourth round of the Milk Cup, 21st December 1982.

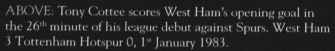

David Cross hits the net for one of his four goals against Spurs, 2nd September 1981.

Giddy Heights

The 1985/6 season proved to be one of the most memorable in West Ham's history. At one point it looked as if the championship trophy could be heading to Green Street. The season ended with West Ham finishing in third place, the highest in their history. And what a journey it was! The season started with some talismanic new signings. Mark Ward joined from Oldham and Frank McAvennie was signed for £340,000 from St Mirren, ostensibly to play in midfield. Both had a huge impact on the team, but it was as a striker where McAvennie thrived, in a prolific partnership with Tony Cottee. The season did not start well, with only two victories in the first eight games. But they then went on a run of 18 games without defeat, including nine successive wins, which saw them rise from 17th to 3rd by mid-December. By Christmas McAvennie had hit the net 17 times and Cottee 10. Phil Parkes was imperious in the West Ham goal, and the back four seemed watertight.

Chelsea 0-4 West Ham.

ABOVE: Chelsea 0-4 West Ham United, 1986 league campaign.

RIGHT: Alan Devonshire holds off an Ipswich Town defender in a fourth round FA Cup tie on 25th January 1986 that ended 0-0. The tie went to a second replay which the Hammers won 1-0 thanks to a Tony Cottee goal. They went out in the quarter-finals away to Sheffield Wednesday.

Dickens scores the West Ham opener in their 2-1 victory against Ipswich, 30th April 1986.

Just Like My Dreams...

Bad weather caused many postponements and eventually the backlog seemed to catch up with West Ham. In April they played three home games in eight days, losing the last one to Chelsea 2-1, even though they had beaten them 4-0 only two weeks earlier at Stamford Bridge. On 21st April West Ham scored a memorable 8-1 victory over Newcastle, which included the bizarre sight of Alvin Martin scoring a hat-trick. This win came in the middle of a run of six successive victories leading to many a Hammers fan dreaming of topping the league. By the end of the season Liverpool had clinched the championship, but second place was still within reach; in the end, however, it was Everton who clinched the runners-up position, beating the Hammers 3-1 in the final match of the season.

West Ham v Ipswich, 30th April 1986.

179

The Boys of '86

Only 18 players were used during the season, but the fact that nine of them played 38 games or more demonstrates how important a constant line-up was to the team. Both Cottee and McAvennie only missed one game, with Cottee scoring 20 goals and McAvennie 26. But it was the back five of Parkes, Gale, Stewart, Martin and Walford who deserve equal acclaim. It had been a tremendous campaign, which is personified by those who the fans came to know as the Boys of '86.

THE BOYS OF '86

Tony Cottee 41 (20)
Alan Devonshire 38 (3)
Alan Dickens 40 (4)
Tony Gale 42
Frank McAvennie 41 (26)
Alvin Martin 40 (4)
Neil Orr 33 (2)
Phil Parkes 42
George Parris 23 (1)
Geoff Pike 10
Ray Stewart 39 (6)
Steve Walford 27
Mark Ward 42 (3)

FAR LEFT: Frank McAvennie.

LEFT: Cottee and McAvennie.

RIGHT: Phil Parkes.

BELOW: Ray Stewart tonks home a winning penalty in the dying minutes. West Ham 2 Ipswich 1, 30th April 1986.

–LEGENDS–

Frank McAvennie

It's not many players who in their last game for a club come off the subs bench and score a hat-trick. But that's what Frank McAvennie did in his final game at Upton Park against Nottingham Forest on 2nd May 1992. If anything was needed to confirm his legendary status, that was it. McAvennie first joined West Ham at the start of the close season in 1985 from St Mirren. He was expected to play in midfield but an injury to Paul Goddard saw him move up front and he never looked back, scoring twice on his home debut. His 26 league goals propelled West Ham to their third-place finish that season. He wasn't just a goalscorer though. His industriousness, tackling and creative abilities were appreciated by all who saw him that season. Hammers fans were shocked to the core when he was sold to Celtic in late 1987, but all was not lost. He returned to Upton Park in May 1989, and although he was never the same player he remained a cult hero.

Frank McAvennie with *EastEnders* stars Gillian Taylforth and Anita Dobson.

Scorecard:

1985-86	51-28
1986-87	47-11
1987-88	9-0
1988-89	9-0
1989-90	5-0
1990-91	39-11
1991-92	31-10

FOOTBALL –STATS–

Frank McAvennie

Name: Francis McAvennie

Born: Glasgow, 22nd December 1959

Position: Striker

West Ham Playing Career: 1985-87, 1989-92

Club Appearances: 191

Goals: 60

Scotland Appearances: 5

Goals: 1

–LEGENDS–

Tony Cottee

Tony Cottee made an immediate impact when he broke into the West Ham first team at the age of 17. If you want the fans on your side it doesn't get much better than scoring against Tottenham on your debut. That was on 1st January 1983. In total that season Cottee made nine appearances, scoring five goals in the process. But it was in the 1985/6 season that Cottee came into his own, scoring 20 league goals in a partnership with Frank McAvennie which took the First Division by storm and saw the Hammers finish in third place. The next season got better and Cottee bagged 22 more. It was inevitable that other clubs would come in for him and, sure enough, he secured a big money move to Everton in August 1988 for a then British record fee of £2.2 million. Naturally enough he scored a hat-trick on his debut. Six years later Harry Redknapp re-signed him to boost a flagging Hammers strike force. The goal machine was well and truly working and he managed a further 24 goals in 69 league appearances before leaving Upton Park for a succession of lower league sides, including Leicester, Norwich and Barnet. It was criminal TC only won seven England caps. He remains the most prolific West Ham striker of the last 30 years.

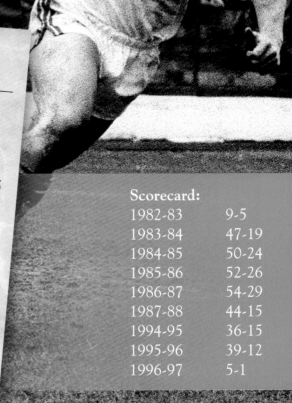

FOOTBALL –STATS–

Tony Cottee

Name: Anthony Richard Cottee

Born: Plaistow, 11th July 1965

Position: Striker

West Ham Playing Career: 1983-88, 1994-96

Club Appearances: 336

Goals: 146

England Appearances: 7

Goals: 0

Scorecard:

1982-83	9-5
1983-84	47-19
1984-85	50-24
1985-86	52-26
1986-87	54-29
1987-88	44-15
1994-95	36-15
1995-96	39-12
1996-97	5-1

Fading & Dying

Having finished third in the league in 1986, West Ham fans were hoping that this time their dreams wouldn't just fade and die, that the club would invest in the future and ensure that West Ham would be challengers for years to come. Instead, the Boys of '86 were broken up with Neil Orr leaving for Hibernian, Frank McAvennie poached by Celtic and Tony Cottee leaving for Everton. David Kelly was signed from Walsall to replace Cottee and an unknown defender from Birmingham, Julian Dicks, was drafted in to the Hammers defence. The 1988/9 season started badly and by the end of October it was clear that relegation was on the cards. There were constant rumours about John Lyall's future. Things didn't improve at Christmas, West Ham were rooted to the bottom of the table. Injuries ravaged the team and led to a single victory in nine home league games at the start of 1989. At Easter John Lyall re-signed Frank McAvennie, who failed to score in any of the eight matches he played in before getting injured. As in previous campaigns where relegation had threatened, West Ham put together a good run on wins towards the end of the season, winning five out of six games. But the last four games of the season were away from home. It proved too much and Liverpool, still chasing the championship, put in a brilliant performance to relegate West Ham with a 5-1 victory at Anfield on West Ham's last day of the season. And it also proved the end of John Lyall's 14-year reign as West Ham manager. He was summarily dismissed, although it was said that the West Ham Board was far from unanimous in the decision.

BELOW LEFT: Tony Cottee escapes from Sheffield Wednesday defenders, 7th November 1987.

RIGHT INSET: Billy Bonds welcomes Liam Brady back to English football, after playing for seven years in Italy. He played 90 games for West Ham, scoring nine goals, 13th March 1987.

BELOW: West Ham 4 Liverpool 1, Littlewoods Cup fourth round, 30th November 1988.

184

John Lyall – a Hammers Great

John Lyall's sacking in June 1989 brought to an end a 34-year association with West Ham United. Discovered by chief scout Wally St Pier, Lyall joined the club as a groundstaff boy in October 1955. He played for the youth team at left-back and played in the 1957 Youth Cup final which West Ham lost 8-2 to Manchester United. He made his full debut in April 1959 but his career was cruelly cut short in 1964 when he was forced into retirement because of a serious knee injury. He then joined the youth team coaching set-up where he greatly impressed Ron Greenwood, who promoted him through the ranks. In September 1974 the club announced that Ron Greenwood would be taking on a new role and John Lyall was given the job of first-team manager.

Success was immediate with a Cup final win at the end of his first season and a European final appearance a year later. Although the club was relegated in 1978 Lyall led the team to another FA Cup win in 1980, followed a year later by a League Cup final appearance and a return to the top flight as Second Division champions. Five years later the club finished third in the league, their highest ever league position. That was the pinnacle of John Lyall's career, but only three years later he lost his job after relegation to the Second Division. A year later he became manager of Ipswich Town, a job he held for four years.

John died suddenly on 18th April 2006, at the age of 66. A minute's silence was held when West Ham played Middlesbrough in the FA Cup final five days later. The silence was broken when the crowd broke into a spontaneous chant of 'Johnny Lyall's Claret and Blue Army'.

He really was a Hammers great, and remains West Ham's most successful manager to date.

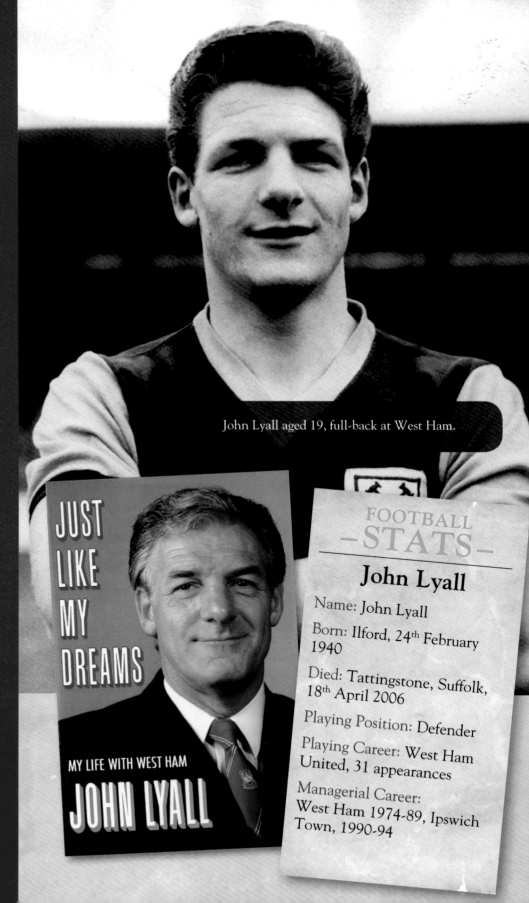

John Lyall aged 19, full-back at West Ham.

JUST LIKE MY DREAMS

MY LIFE WITH WEST HAM

JOHN LYALL

FOOTBALL – STATS –

John Lyall

Name: John Lyall

Born: Ilford, 24th February 1940

Died: Tattingstone, Suffolk, 18th April 2006

Playing Position: Defender

Playing Career: West Ham United, 31 appearances

Managerial Career: West Ham 1974-89, Ipswich Town, 1990-94

John Lyall watching a game with Billy Bonds.

Before the Premier League –
1989-93

RIGHT: From left to right: Alvin Martin, Clive Allen,
Tony Gale, Julian Dicks, Steve Potts, Stuart Slater.

The Lou Macari Era
1989-1990

Former Celtic and Manchester United striker Lou Macari was recruited in the summer of 1989 to take over as team manager. From the outset there was trouble. The players didn't respond well to the new fitness regime and more direct style of play. Midfield maestro Alan Dickens left for Chelsea and Paul Ince instantly became a Hammers hate figure when he was pictured in a Manchester United shirt having pulled out of the club's pre-season tour of Sweden. Mark Ward was transferred to Manchester City in a deal which saw Trevor Morley and Ian Bishop coming the other way. Jimmy Quinn, Martin Allen, Colin Foster and Czech goalkeeper Ludek Miklosko were also signed. It really did seem the dawn of a new era but results started to go against Macari. He also received very bad publicity in a betting scandal involving his former club Swindon Town, and after a 6-0 away defeat at Oldham the vultures were circling. Macari failed to show up for an away game at Swindon and his resignation was accepted the next day. The Macari era had lasted a mere 229 days.

> " *I was crazy to resign like that because looking back, and knowing what football is like today, I suppose it really was no more than a storm in a teacup.*
>
> Lou Macari

Lou Macari pictured at Upton Park at the start of his job as manager of West Ham, 7th July 1989.

Julian Dicks sent off during the West Ham v Wimbledon game on 23rd November 1989.

Martin Allen scores West Ham's opener in a 5-0 thumping of Sunderland, 18th October 1989.

> "I found it impossible to believe how the club could employ someone who had gambled against his own team and I just found it impossible to play for him."
>
> Mark Ward

The Billy Bonds Era
1990-1994

Billy Bonds received a rousing reception from West Ham fans whose relief at the departure of the hapless Macari was palpable. He appointed Hammers stalwart Ronnie Boyce as his number two. A good run of results saw the Hammers just miss out on a play-off place. The following season, 1990/1, proved rather more successful. Bonds brought in Tim Breacker at right-back, Chris Hughton at left-back as cover for Julian Dicks, and Iain Dowie up front. But it was winger Stuart Slater who provided the impetus to what proved to be a promotion-winning season. His performance in the FA Cup quarter-final against Everton was mesmerizing. In the semi-final against Nottingham Forest referee Keith Hackett erroneously sent off Tony Gale for a professional foul. Forest went on to win 4-0 but the match is memorable for the reaction of the West Ham fans who proceeded to chant 'Billy Bonds' Claret and Blue Army' for most of the rest of the game. At the end of the season the Second Division title was in West Ham's grasp, but a 2-1 home defeat to Notts County on the final day saw the Hammers finish second to champions Oldham.

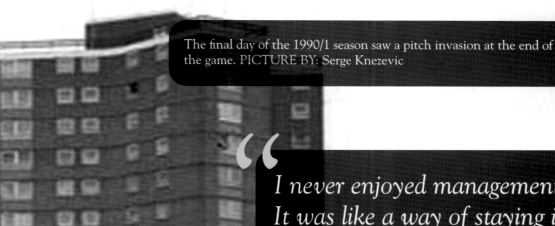

The final day of the 1990/1 season saw a pitch invasion at the end of the game. PICTURE BY: Serge Knezevic

" *I never enjoyed management. It was like a way of staying in the game. But for me, it could never replace playing.*

Billy Bonds "

" *Billy used to start training in the gym an hour before everyone else and I used to do the same in the hope of being as fit as he was. He was first class and the type of person you wanted to play for.*

Mark Ward on Billy Bonds "

'Billy Bonds' Claret and Blue Army'

West Ham reached the semi-final of the FA Cup in 1991 and faced Nottingham Forest at Villa Park on 14th April. Unfortunately, they also faced Keith Hackett. In the 25th minute West Ham stalwart Tony Gale collided with Forest's Gary Crosby. The Forest player was heading away from goal but the referee sent Gale off for a supposed professional foul. West Ham held out until half-time, but in the second half Forest scored four times. Every West Ham fan who was there or watching on TV will remember the constant chanting throughout the second half of 'Billy Bonds' Claret and Blue Army'.

Relegated Again

The cost of implementing the Taylor report and improving safety standards at the Boleyn Ground meant that Bonds had little more than £1 million to spend to improve his squad for the 1991/2 season. It was not enough. Mitchell Thomas, Mike Small and Kenny Brown arrived. Small scored 10 goals by the end of that October, but only scored three more during the whole season. It wasn't only on the pitch where there was trouble. Off it the West Ham Board launched its ill-fated Bond Scheme to try to raise some much needed cash. Fans reacted badly and several on pitch demonstrations were held. At the end of the season West Ham yo-yoed back into Division Two, finishing bottom.

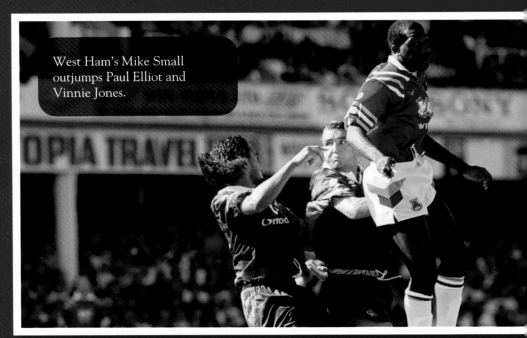

West Ham's Mike Small outjumps Paul Elliot and Vinnie Jones.

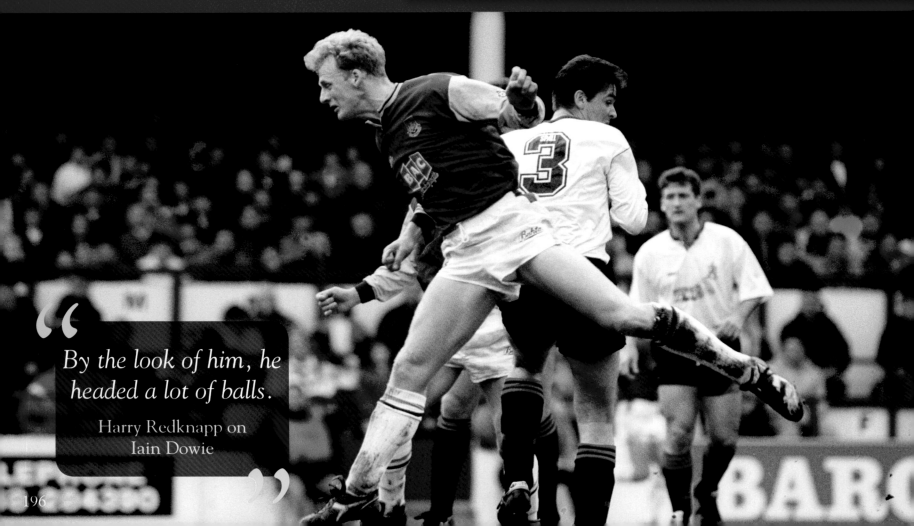

By the look of him, he headed a lot of balls.

Harry Redknapp on
Iain Dowie

Frank McAvennie celebrates scoring against Millwall. And to be frank, who wouldn't? West Ham 3 Millwall 1, 24th February 1991.

–LEGENDS–

Julian Dicks

Julian Dicks signed for West Ham in August 1988 for £300,000 from Birmingham City, where he had established a reputation as a tough-tackling, tenacious defender with a fierce shot. He was – and is – a born leader of men and was given the West Ham captaincy at the start of the 1991/2 season at the age of 23. But in 1993 manager Billy Bonds stripped him of the captaincy after he was sent off three times during the season. When Harry Redknapp took over the writing was on the wall and he was transferred to Liverpool in a swap deal which saw David Burrows and Mike Marsh come the other way. But a year later he returned to Upton Park, having hated his injury-prone time on Merseyside. Between 1990 and 1997 Julian Dicks won Hammer of the Year on four occasions – testament to the high regard supporters had for him. His second stint at West Ham was memorable but also injury hit and in 1999 "The Terminator" was forced to retire because of his persistent knee injury. The fact that he was never picked for England was the country's loss.

Julian Dicks has a *Daily Mirror* football kit painted on to his body during the *Daily Mirror* Pepsi promotion, 1st April 1996.

Scorecard:

1987-88	8-0
1988-89	49-2
1989-90	52-14
1990-91	15-5
1991-92	30-5
1992-93	42-14
1993-94	7-0
1994-95	33-5
1995-96	40-11
1996-97	38-8
1998-99	12-1

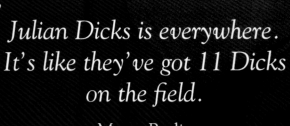

" *Julian Dicks is everywhere. It's like they've got 11 Dicks on the field.*

Metro Radio "

FOOTBALL –STATS–

Julian Dicks

Name: Julian Andrew Dicks

Born: Bristol, 8th August 1968

Position: Left-back

West Ham Playing Career: 1988-93, 1994-99

Club Appearances: 326

Goals: 65

England Appearances: 0

Goals: 0

Promotion 1993

At the start of the 1992/3 season former Hammers winger Harry Redknapp replaced Ronnie Boyce as number two to Billy Bonds.

Star player Stuart Slater was sold to Celtic to raise some much-needed transfer funds. Matty Holmes, Peter Butler and Mark Robson were brought in to boost the Hammers' promotion hopes. The Premier League came into being at the start of the 1992/3 season, but West Ham still languished in Division Two. It was a close-run thing, achieved only on the last day of the season on goal difference from Portsmouth. Mark Robson and Kevin Keen performed wonders on the wings, supplying the ammunition for Trevor Morley to top score with 20 goals and Clive Allen to hit 14 in 25 games. Julian Dicks thundered in 11 goals, but it was also the watertight Hammers' defence of Breacker, Dicks, Potts and Martin that made the difference. Finally, it was time for West Ham to take their rightful place, in the top flight of English football, in the Premier League.

Harry Redknapp and Billy Bonds: a partnership which was to end in acrimony.

SEASON FACTS:
P46 W26 D10 L10 F81 A41 88 **Pts – Position** 2nd
Regular side: L Miklosko, S Potts, A Martin, T Breacker, J Dicks, K Keen, M Robson, P Butler, M Allen, T Morley, C Allen
Top scorers: Trevor Morley 15, Clive Allen 15, Julian Dicks 11
Captain: Julian Dicks
Hammer of the Year: Steve Potts

LEFT: Ludo Miklosko is beaten by a shot from Kerry Dixon.

RIGHT: Mike Small.

Hammers of the Year
1957/8 – 1992/3

1957/8 Andy Malcolm
1958/9 Ken Brown
1959/60 Malcolm Musgrove
1960/1 Bobby Moore
1961/2 Lawrie Leslie
1962/3 Bobby Moore
1963/4 Johnny Byrne
1964/5 Martin Peters
1965/6 Geoff Hurst
1966/7 Geoff Hurst
1967/8 Bobby Moore
1968/9 Geoff Hurst
1969/70 Bobby Moore
1970/1 Billy Bonds
1971/2 Trevor Brooking
1972/3 Bryan Robson
1973/4 Billy Bonds
1974/5 Billy Bonds
1975/6 Trevor Brooking
1976/7 Trevor Brooking
1977/8 Trevor Brooking
1978/9 Alan Devonshire
1979/80 Alvin Martin
1980/1 Phil Parkes
1981/2 Alvin Martin
1982/3 Trevor Brooking
1983/4 Trevor Brooking
1984/5 Paul Allen
1985/6 Tony Cottee
1986/7 Billy Bonds
1987/8 Stewart Robson
1988/9 Paul Ince
1989/90 Julian Dicks
1990/1 Ludek Miklosko
1991/2 Julian Dicks
1992/3 Steve Potts

ABOVE: Tony Cottee in typical scoring pose.

ABOVE LEFT: Paul Allen.

LEFT: Alvin Martin.

It's July 1991 and a pensive Bobby Moore makes a sentimental journey back to Wembley Stadium, the scene of so many of his triumphs.

201

Farewell to a Hero

The 1992/3 season also had its desperately sad moments. All Hammers fans will remember where they were when they heard Bobby Moore had died, succumbing to cancer at the terribly young age of 51. Wednesday 24th February 1993 is a day we all recall. Within minutes of the news of Moore's death, crowds were gathering outside the West Ham gates leaving flowers and scarves. Grown men cried. Strangers hugged each other. It was as if a close member of their family had suddenly died. And in a way they had. The loss was felt by everyone associated with the club, however loosely.

"Bobby Moore was simply the greatest footballer ever to have graced the Academy of Football."

"We still miss him today."

For many years he delighted supporters of West Ham and was a formidable opponent in the eyes of those against whom he played. But it is for his appearances for England – ninety of them as captain – that he will be chiefly remembered, and supremely for his captaincy of the World Cup team of 1966.

Dean of Westminster

Westminster Abbey

A Service of Thanksgiving for the Life of Bobby Moore OBE
1941-1993

Monday 28 June 1993

Noon

> "He was my friend as well as the greatest defender I ever played against. The world has lost one of its greatest football players and an honourable gentleman."
>
> Pelé

The Bobby Moore statue, sculpted by Philip Jackson, outside the new Wembley Stadium. Picture by Gareth Fogg, taken in December 2010.

Dedicated to my friends John Parry, Paul Joliffe and Jo Phillips, the inhabitants of seats X200-203,
next to me in the West Stand.
And to Viv Archer, who will sell hundreds of copies of this book in the excellent Newham Bookshop in Barking Road.
At least, she'd better.

MirrorPix Photographic Research – Alex Waters, David Scripps, John Mead, Vito Inglese and Manjit Sandhu.
Newham Archives Photographic Research by Jenni Munro-Collins.

I'd like to thank Tony Hogg and John Helliar for their magnificent books which have provided many of the statistics quoted in
this book – *Who's Who of West Ham United* and *West Ham United: The Elite Era*.

Particular thanks go to John Northcutt for his invaluable help and advice during the compilation of this book,
and to www.westhamstats.info for providing the majority of the statistics used.

Thanks also to Grant Tucker who has learned more about West Ham than he probably ever wanted to know.
But has now become a supporter, so there's lovely (he's Welsh, by the way).

And to Richard Havers, the series editor of When Football Was Football,
who had the foresight to ask me to compile this book.